A Student's Guide to Studying the Bible

Tommy Lea & Ann B. Cannon

LifeWay Press
Nashville, Tennessee

© Copyright 2000 • LifeWay Press
All rights reserved
ISBN 0-6330-0454-5

This book is based on the out-of-print book *A Guide for the Journey: Survival Kit 3, Youth Edition.*

This book is the text for course number CG-0561
in the subject area "Bible Studies-Youth" in the
Christian Growth category of the Christian Growth Study Plan.

Dewey Classification Number: 220.07
Subject HEADING: BIBLE–STUDY and TEACHING\YOUTH–RELIGIOUS LIFE

Unless indicated otherwise, all Scripture quotations are from the Holy Bible, *New International Version,* copyright © 1973, 1978, 1984 by International Bible Society.

Printed in the United States of America
Available from LifeWay Church Resources Customer Service, 1-800-458-2772
and Lifeway Christian Stores.

Cover Illustration: Hilber Nelson
Art Direction & Design: Edward Crawford

Youth Section
Discipleship and Family Group
LifeWay Christian Resources of the Southern Baptist Convention
127 Ninth Avenue, North
Nashville, TN 37234-0152

Contents

The Writers 4

Introduction 5

Week 1: Are You Ready? 6

Week 2: One Bible Study Prerequisite 21

Week 3: Two Rules to Guide Bible Study 36

Week 4: Three Ways to Do Bible Study 52

Week 5: Four Areas to Apply Bible Study 68

Week 6: Five Helps in Doing Bible Study 84

Group Learning Activities 101

Scripture Memory Cards 109

Christian Growth Study Plan 111

The Writers

Tommy Lea went home to be with his Lord on July 2, 1999 after a four-and-a half year battle with cancer. He was a graduate of Mississippi State University, responding to God's call on his life during his senior year. He earned a master of divinity and a doctor of theology at Southwestern Baptist Theological Seminary. He was named the dean of the theology school at Southwestern in 1995 where he had served as a professor of New Testament since 1979. Prior to coming to Southwestern, Lea served as pastor in Alabama, Virginia, and Texas. His favorite Scripture passage was *Lamentations 3:22-23, Because of the Lord's great love we are not consumed, for his compassions never fail. They are new every morning; great is your faithfulness.* He is survived by his wife, Beverly, three children, and five grandchildren.

Ann B. Cannon can be defined by her work—18 books for students, workers and parents, 25 years of writing curriculum Bible studies, conference leading throughout the United States and abroad, more than 30 years as a volunteer youth worker at Wieuca Road Baptist Church in Atlanta, Georgia. She can also be defined by her interests—fanatical fan of the Atlanta Braves, avid reader, and lover of places in the mountains or beside the ocean. But, she most likes to be known as the wife of Cecil and the mother of her adult children, Corey and Casey, all of whom give her a peaceful sense that she is truly blessed.

Introduction

DO YOU WANT TO KNOW...
- who "Pharaoh, Pharaoh" really is, is?
- what *propitiation* means?
- why Job had to suffer?
- what the Bible says about kissing?
- who were the first animal rights activists in the Bible?

Great! You've picked the right book. Answers to all these questions and more are found in the Bible. All you need are the right keys to help you to discover the truths in the Bible. During the next six weeks you will learn basic skills and identify those keys. You will learn how to:
- examine an entire book of the Bible or a single biblical passage;
- study a Bible person or a specific trait found in several people of the Bible;
- investigate the history, geography, and culture behind a specific Bible passage;
- let the language of the Bible help you interpret a Scripture;
- look at a specific topic in the Bible;
- evaluate the theology of a Bible passage;
- apply Bible verses to your daily life.

In addition to learning how to study the Bible, you will memorize Scripture verses related to your studies. (Don't panic! This will be easier than you think!)

GETTING WITH THE PLAN
To make it through six weeks of study you need a plan. Each week contains five days of study material. Each day's material will take you 20 to 30 minutes to complete. Each day you will use your Bible, as well as complete the research and response activities in this workbook.

Stop and make a plan. The information below will help you. OK, let's get going.

MY PLAN
I will set aside time each day for this study at _____(time)
in_____ (location) .
My accountability partner is _____
I will participate in the group study at _____
(time and place of your group meetings).
Sign your name as a personal commitment to stick with the plan.

_____(signature)

Week 1
Are You Ready?

This Week's Scripture Memory Passage
The law of the Lord is perfect, reviving the soul. The statutes of the Lord are trustworthy, making wise the simple. The precepts of the Lord are right, giving joy to the heart. The commands of the Lord are radiant, giving light to the eyes (Ps. 19:7-8).

This Week's Lessons
Day 1: Ready for Action?
Day 2: Ready to Memorize?
Day 3: Ready to Translate?
Day 4: Ready to Research?
Day 5: Ready to Get Started?

This week you will:
- overview the six-week study;
- evaluate the importance of memorizing, and learn ways to memorize each week's Scripture memory passage;
- look at the value of modern Bible translations and paraphrases;
- examine different study tools to help you study the Bible;
- check out several possible passages for Bible study.

This Week's Bible Study Tip
Each week you will learn a variety of different Bible study methods. Along with these methods, you will look at how to develop good Bible study habits. To help you remember all this information, use the fingers on your hand. Each finger will represent one week's study. You will label the fingers to help you remember what you've studied. For example, the thumb will remind you of week 2's study titled One Bible Study Prerequisite. The remaining fingers will relate to the Bible study ideas and methods you study in weeks 3, 4, 5, and 6.

Take time now to draw your hand on the front inside page of this book. If your hand is too big for the page, find a friend with a smaller hand to use for your drawing. Every week you'll label this drawing, so be sure to draw a hand big enough to write on.

By the time you finish this six-week study, you can look at your hand and recall the methods you've learned. You should also be able to repeat the Scripture memory passage you will learn each week.

ARE YOU READY?

Day 1
Ready for Action!

Read and mark *Psalm 19:7-8* in your Bible. Use your Scripture memory passage card to begin memorizing *Psalm 19:7-8.*

Congratulations! Here you are on day 1 of week 1. You have a brand-new workbook and are ready to go. In the next six weeks you will discover ways to give new life and deeper meaning to your personal Bible study.

WARNING!! Satan doesn't want you to learn more about God. He will try to throw you off track. Check the distractions that might take you away from your daily commitment to this study.
- ❏ tons of homework to do
- ❏ catching up on sleep
- ❏ starting another project
- ❏ doing an errand for mom
- ❏ a friend calls
- ❏ going out with a friend
- ❏ attending a church event
- ❏ doing your regular chores

None of these distractions are bad, but Satan may use these to tempt you from a regular Bible study time. You skip one day, then a second, and suddenly you're a week behind. Don't let that happen. Be smart! Stick with your commitment to this study. Let friends in your study group keep you accountable.

DIGGING IN!
Did you read this week's introduction? Every week the introductory page tells you what that week's Scripture memory passage is. It offers an overview of the five days of study. You will also find a helpful Bible study tip. If you skipped the introductory stuff for this week, I'll wait here until you get back.

Welcome back! That didn't take long. What was this week's Bible study tip?

_____

(Oops! Almost forgot. You always will need a writing utensil to pen in your responses. I assume you also have your Bible.)

Each week you will examine Bible study techniques, methods, and tricks. Today you will overview the complete, six-week study and become familiar with this book.

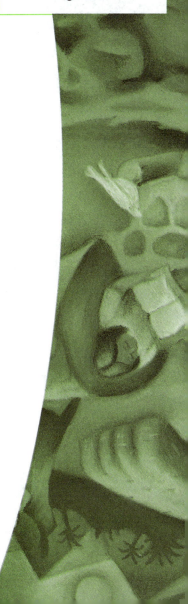

A STUDENT'S GUIDE TO STUDYING THE BIBLE

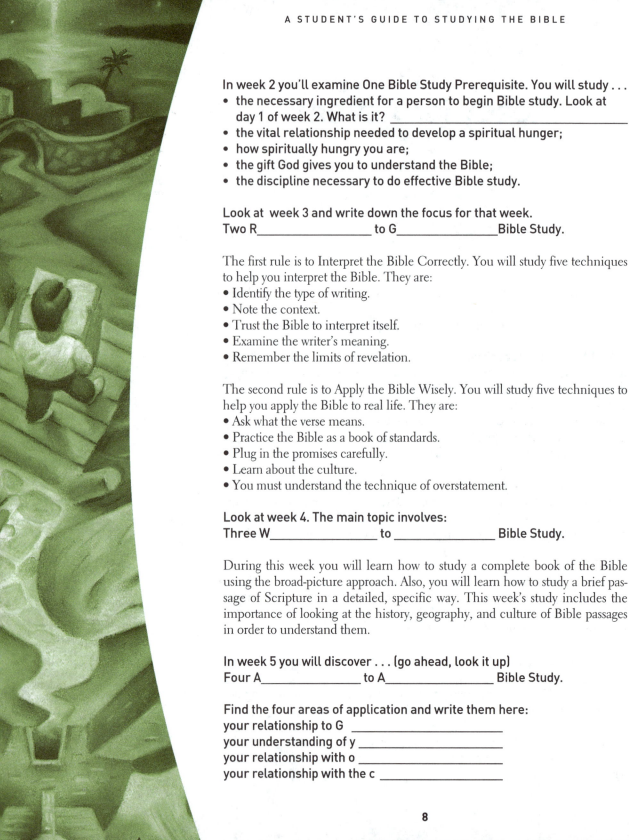

In week 2 you'll examine One Bible Study Prerequisite. You will study . . .
- the necessary ingredient for a person to begin Bible study. Look at day 1 of week 2. What is it? _____
- the vital relationship needed to develop a spiritual hunger;
- how spiritually hungry you are;
- the gift God gives you to understand the Bible;
- the discipline necessary to do effective Bible study.

Look at week 3 and write down the focus for that week.
Two R_____ to G_____ Bible Study.

The first rule is to Interpret the Bible Correctly. You will study five techniques to help you interpret the Bible. They are:
- Identify the type of writing.
- Note the context.
- Trust the Bible to interpret itself.
- Examine the writer's meaning.
- Remember the limits of revelation.

The second rule is to Apply the Bible Wisely. You will study five techniques to help you apply the Bible to real life. They are:
- Ask what the verse means.
- Practice the Bible as a book of standards.
- Plug in the promises carefully.
- Learn about the culture.
- You must understand the technique of overstatement.

Look at week 4. The main topic involves:
Three W_____ to _____ Bible Study.

During this week you will learn how to study a complete book of the Bible using the broad-picture approach. Also, you will learn how to study a brief passage of Scripture in a detailed, specific way. This week's study includes the importance of looking at the history, geography, and culture of Bible passages in order to understand them.

In week 5 you will discover . . . (go ahead, look it up)
Four A_____ to A_____ Bible Study.

Find the four areas of application and write them here:
your relationship to G _____
your understanding of y _____
your relationship with o _____
your relationship with the c _____

ARE YOU READY?

As you look at these four relationships you also will be studying three more methods to use in Bible study. You will apply each day's Bible study to these four areas.

Week 6 may feel like English lessons, instead of Bible study helps, but you will study... Five_____in_____Bible Study.

Words, figures of speech, and grammar form the first three days of study. On the last two days you will look at topics and doctrines. (Don't worry, by then you'll understand what all this means.)

Your hand diagram in the front of the book is a reminder of each week's contents. As you review each week's topic, check out each week's introduction and write down the Bible reference for that week's Scripture memory passage.

The thumb stands for One Bible Study Prerequisite. To do effective Bible study you must be a spiritually hungry child of God.

The Scripture memory passage reference is _____.

The first finger represents Two Rules to Guide Bible Study. You will use guidelines to interpret the Bible and to apply its message.

The Scripture memory passage reference is_____.

The middle finger stands for Three Ways to Do Bible Study. You will look at different methods for studying the Bible.

The Scripture memory passage reference is_____.

The ring finger is for Four Areas to Apply Bible study. You will apply biblical teachings to your own life and to your relationships.

The Scripture memory passage reference is _____.

The small finger represents Five Helps in Doing Bible Study. You will learn how to interpret the words, figures of speech, grammar, topics, and doctrines of the Bible.

The Scripture memory passage reference is_____.

Whew! Congratulations! You made it through your first day!

Day 2
Ready to Memorize?

Yesterday you began working on memorizing your first week's Scripture memory passage which is *Psalm* 19:7-8. In the margin write the verses, copying them from your Bible or from the Scripture memory card.

Every week you will memorize a new Scripture passage. You may see this as a challenge or as a nuisance.

What keeps you from memorizing Scripture? (Check all that apply.)
❑ I have trouble memorizing anything
❑ I can't stay focused
❑ It reminds me of school
❑ I don't understand why I have to memorize anything
❑ It's too hard
❑ I don't like memorizing Scripture
❑ I'm basically lazy
❑ I've never tried it

Most of us, if we're honest, will admit that we're basically too lazy to memorize Scripture. But, during these next six weeks, I hope you'll take the challenge and learn six new Scripture passages. Each week remove the Scripture memory passage card for that week from this book. Carry the card with you during the week. Work on memorizing every chance you have. You'll be surprised how many times you can work on memorizing during a day.

Why do you think memorizing Scripture is a vital part of learning how to study the Bible? (Check all that apply.)
❑ to be able to use Scripture when I pray
❑ to earn points with the Bible study teacher
❑ to be able to recall verses when things go wrong in my life
❑ to impress my friends
❑ to remind me of God's best when I am tempted to sin
❑ to help me mature spiritually

ARE YOU READY?

Whatever your reasons, keep memorizing. You can overcome the negative thoughts about memory work by just doing it. Here are some ideas to help you memorize these passages.

First, use a Bible translation in language that you understand. This book uses the *New International Version* (NIV). Each Bible translation is a little different. Once you learn a Scripture in one translation, it may sound different in another. Use the same translation during all six weeks of study.

Second, get a friend to work with you. That way you have someone to challenge you. Make it a friendly competition to see who can memorize the Scripture memory passage first each week.

WAYS TO MEMORIZE SCRIPTURE
Some people can read a Scripture several times, and repeat it back without missing a word. Others struggle. Try these ideas to help make your Scripture memory work a little easier.
- *Make up a tune to go with the verse.* We tend to remember the words of songs. If you are memorizing a psalm, it will be easy to put the verses to music because the psalms were originally songs.
- *Make flash cards of key words from the verse.* When you work on memorizing, use these cards to remind you of key words in the passage. As you learn the verse, you can use fewer flash cards.
- *Write out the verbs in the verse(s) on a reminder card.* Do the same with the *nouns* in the verse. Use these cards as you start memorizing.
- *Summarize the verse in your own words* to show your understanding of it.
- *Figure out how the verse relates to your life.*

OK, let's try these ideas on this week's Scripture memory passage from the NIV in the margin to the right.

The law of the Lord is perfect, reviving the soul. The statutes of the Lord are trustworthy, making wise the simple. The precepts of the Lord are right, giving joy to the heart. The commands of the Lord are radiant, giving light to the eyes (Ps. 19:7-8).

The psalmist emphasized the importance of Scripture. God can use Scripture to revive us, to give us wisdom, to provide us joy, and to open our eyes spiritually. Again, in the margin, write a summary of these verses, in your own words.

Use a match-up as you continue to understand the passage. Match the first phrase (1, 2, 3, or 4) with the related results (a, b, c, or d).
____ 1. The law of the Lord is perfect,
____ 2. The statutes of the Lord are trustworthy,
____ 3. The precepts of the Lord are right,
____ 4. The commands of the Lord are radiant,

a. making wise the simple.   b. giving joy to the heart.
c. giving light to the eyes.   d. reviving the soul.

A STUDENT'S GUIDE TO STUDYING THE BIBLE

What are the main verbs in these verses? _____
_____

What are the main nouns in these verses? _____
_____

Write the verse in the margin of this book.

If you enjoy memorizing Scripture, here are additional verses.
- *Matthew 18:15*   • *John 13:34-35*
- *Acts 17:11*   • *Ephesians 4:32*
- *Philippians 3:10* • *Hebrews 12:14*

Day 3
Ready to Translate?

WORDS EVERYWHERE!
Write a brief definition beside the following words:
dough _____
phat _____
web _____
chick _____
ram _____
dis _____

Did you define *dough* as a mixture of flour, liquid and shortening or as money? Is *phat* a misspelled synonym for obesity? Does a spider design a *web* or is this the computer equivalent of outer space? Is a *chick* a baby fowl or a girl? Did you call a *ram* a male sheep with horns or a computer's memory? And, does *dis* have any other meaning than to talk negatively about a person? Words change, don't they?

The Bible is like that. The words used in one way in the Bible sound strange in today's world. The original Bible texts written in Hebrew for the Old Testament and Greek for the New Testament were lost long ago.

Through the centuries scribes faithfully copied the holy verses. (Remember, this was before the printing press came on the scene.) When some versions of the Bible were translated, the translators relied on the oldest texts that were available. For example, the *King James Version* was written in 1611 using early English translations of the Bible, as well as the oldest-known manuscripts in Hebrew and Greek.

Many people prefer the *King James Version* because of its picturesque language. If you prefer Shakespeare to Steinbech you may very well prefer the *King James Version*. It was also one of the earliest Bible translations available to the masses of everyday people.

Today's Bible translations have several advantages over older translations:
- Newer translations are based on older manuscripts located after these earlier translated editions of the Bible. These older manuscripts provide more accurate information because they were closer to the original manuscripts that have been lost.
- Advanced biblical scholarship makes today's translations more accurate. God continues to bless us with tools and persons who know how to use those tools to better understand His truths found in Scripture.
- Modern translations are written in paragraph form making it easier to read. Likewise, poetry is printed in poetic style, so it can be easily identified from the rest of the text.
- Modern translations use the language of today.

What translation(s) of the Bible do you have?_____
_____

TRANSLATIONS EVERYWHERE!
First, learn the difference between a paraphrase and a translation. A translation takes the original Greek and Hebrew languages and accurately puts these into a readable form. These translations stay faithful to the original languages. Awkward expressions or confusing sentence structure can make translating some passages difficult. Bible translations are similar to your translating a sentence from Spanish into English.

A paraphrase also uses the oldest Greek and Hebrew text, but this editor seeks to express the thoughts and emotions behind the language. Paraphrases are easy to read. However, it is dangerous to build a theology on a paraphrase since the paraphrase is less formal than a translation. A paraphrase would be similar to your taking a Spanish text and writing your idea of what the author was trying to say, rather than a word-for-word translation.

What factors are important to you in selecting a translation?
- ❑ It's written in words I can understand.
- ❑ I look for accuracy in a translation.
- ❑ It's a translation that my friends use.
- ❑ It has a nice cover on the Bible.
- ❑ I like the flow of the language.
- ❑ It's the translation I've always used.
- ❑ It's the translation my parents used.
- ❑ It's the least expensive Bible I could find.

Let's see how Bible translations and paraphrases compare. Locate *John 3:16* in your Bible. In the margin of this book copy *John 3:16* from your Bible. Now look at the same verse as written in different translations. Note how each translator arranged the words and thoughts.

For God so loved the world, that he gave his only begotten Son, that whosoever believeth in him should not perish, but have everlasting life (KJV).[1]

For God so loved the world that he gave his only Son, that whoever believes in him should not perish but have eternal life (RSV).[2]

For God loved the world so much that he gave his only Son, so that everyone who believes in him may not die but have eternal life (GNB).[3]

For God so loved the world, that He gave His only begotten Son, that whoever believes in Him should not perish, but have eternal life (NASB).[4]

God loved the people of this world so much that he gave his only Son, so that everyone who has faith in him will have eternal life and never really die (CEV).[5]

For God so loved the world that he gave his one and only Son, that whoever believes in him shall not perish but have eternal life (NIV).

Here is the same verse from three paraphrased Bibles.

For God loved the world so much that he gave his only Son, so that anyone who believes in him shall not perish but have eternal life(TLB).[6]

"This is how much God loved the world: He gave his Son, his one and only Son. And this is why: so that no one need be destroyed; by believing in him, anyone can have a whole and lasting life" (The Message by Eugene H. Patterson).[7]

"For God loved the world so much that He gave His Only Son, so that anyone who trusts in Him may never perish but have eternal life" (Williams New Testament, *The New Testament in the Language of the People*).⁸

If possible, use two or three translations as you work on a Bible study. You'll find each translation adds unique insight to your study. You may find a Bible that is designed with three or four translations in parallel columns for comparison. Some Bible translations like the *New International Version* also come on a computer CD with Bible study notes.

There is one more Bible book you might find helpful. It is *A Harmony of the Synoptic Gospels*. The synoptic Gospels are the first three gospels of the New Testament—Matthew, Mark, and Luke. Because these gospels used the same sources when they were written, they tend to have parallel passages. In a Harmony, the similar passages are listed side by side so you can compare each story, parable, or verse without flipping to each gospel. This Harmony uses the New American Standard.

Day 4
Ready to Research?

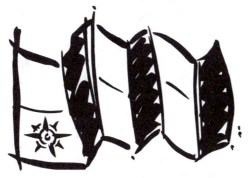

How is your memory work on this week's Scripture memory passage? Write *Psalm 19:7-8* in the margin. If you are still struggling, look back to day 2, and select one way to help you memorize these verses.

You may have difficulty understanding some passages of Scripture. Fortunately, scholars who love the Bible have produced biblical resources for those of us who need help. Today, let's look at the various Bible helps available to someone who wants to study and understand the Bible.

A STUDENT'S GUIDE TO STUDYING THE BIBLE

WHAT'S AVAILABLE
Test what you know about Bible study resources by matching the definition with the study help. Look for the answers in today's study.
____ 1. A Bible dictionary
____ 2. A Bible concordance
____ 3. A Bible commentary
____ 4. A lexicon
____ 5. A Bible encyclopedia
____ 6. A topical Bible
____ 7. A Bible atlas
____ 8. A Bible translation
____ 9. A Bible paraphrase

a. takes the language of the Bible and restates it in the language of today, staying faithful to the original language and content.
b. a dictionary that deals with the original languages; Hebrew for the Old Testament and Greek for the New Testament.
c. arranged by topics, identifying all verses related to that topic.
d. gives detailed information about words, people, places, and events mentioned in the Bible.
e. offers detailed explanations of Scripture passages.
f. takes the language of the Bible and restates it in a more informal translation that includes emotions and interpretations.
g. a resource that explains the background, culture, archeology, and theology of biblical times.
h. alphabetically lists words in the Bible, along with a brief phrase using the word, and the reference in the form "book, chapter, verse."
i. contains maps identifying the land and what it was called during the different periods of the Bible.

In a *Bible dictionary* you can find out who Abigail was, what the names of God are, what a leviathan probably was, and the layout of Solomon's temple. A Bible dictionary gives detailed information about words, people, places, and events mentioned in the Bible. Some Bible dictionaries are rather hefty; others are published in paperback. An excellent Bible dictionary written for students is the *Holman Student Bible Dictionary* by Karen Dockrey, and Johnnie and Phyllis Godwin. (The answer to *1* is *d*.)

A *Bible concordance* shows you how many references there are in the Bible to *gourds* (two) and where they are *(1 Kings 6:18; 2 Kings 4:39)*. If you look up a more common word like *day,* you will find more than 100 references. A concordance alphabetically lists words in the Bible, along with a brief phrase using the word, and the Bible reference. An exhaustive concordance will list every word in the Bible and its reference, making for a very thick book. Most concordances, however, focus on key words in the Bible. (The answer to *2* is *h*.)

ARE YOU READY?

A *Bible commentary* offers detailed explanations of Scripture passages in a one-volume edition or a multi-volume set. Some commentaries like the one-volume *International Bible Commentary* edited by F. F. Bruce contain brief explanations about the Scripture. A commentary like *The Broadman Bible Commentary* has twelve volumes and a fuller explanation of Bible books and passages. (The answer to 3 is *e*.)

A *lexicon* is for serious students. Unless you can read Hebrew or Greek, you won't need a lexicon which deals with the original languages of the Old and New Testaments. But now you know what a lexicon is. (The answer to 4 is *b*.)

A *Bible encyclopedia* is like other encyclopedias, containing a variety of information about the background, culture, archeology, and theology of biblical times. You can find out what musical instruments were played in biblical times or study a time line that links together the Old Testament stories. *Nelson's Illustrated Encyclopedia of the Bible*, edited by John Drane has a diversity of information. (The answer to 5 is *g*.)

A *topical Bible* is similar to a concordance, but it is arranged by topics, identifying all verses related to that topic. In addition to listing words, it also lists phrases like "Blessing—Responsive Blessings of the Law." *So That's in the Bible?* published by Broadman & Holman combines the information in a concordance and a topical Bible, offering Scripture references on a wide variety of topics from advertising to fashions to *Dodo*. (The answer to 6 is *c*.)

A *Bible atlas* contains maps identifying the land and what it was called during the different periods of the Bible. Sometimes maps are included in another book like an encyclopedia. By comparing a map of Paul's world to a map of today, you can see the modern-day countries where Paul took the good news of Jesus Christ. (The answer to 7 is *i*.)

Yesterday you studied the difference in *Bible translations* and *Bible paraphrases*. Did you remember that a translation takes the language of the Bible and restates it in the language of today, staying faithful to the original language and content? Did you also remember that a paraphrase takes the language of the Bible and restates it into a more informal translation that includes emotions and interpretations? (The answer to 8 is *a* and the answer to 9 is *f*.)

WHERE TO FIND THESE RESOURCES
It is highly unlikely that you have all these Bible study helps at home. However, you might have more than you think. Start with the back of your Bible. Check the helps you find there.

- ❑ a word list (Bible dictionary)
- ❑ a time line
- ❑ maps (Bible atlas)
- ❑ a concordance
- ❑ descriptions of Bible books
- ❑ teachings of Jesus
- ❑ what else? _____

A STUDENT'S GUIDE TO STUDYING THE BIBLE

OK, that's a start. Now, look around your house. Maybe your parent, brother, or sister has Bible study helps. (You never know until you ask.) What is available at your house? Check those helps you find.
- ❏ Bible dictionary
- ❏ Bible commentary
- ❏ topical Bible
- ❏ Bible concordance
- ❏ Bible encyclopedia
- ❏ Bible atlas

Finally, you might look in your church's Media Center or library. Check out a book and see how often you use it in Bible study. If you use it often, you might consider buying your own. If you don't use it often, borrow it only when you need it. Check at public libraries, also.

If you are Internet active, there are numerous websites that offer Bible study helps. If you want more Internet information, turn to "This Week's Bible Study Tip" for week 5.

HOW TO USE THESE RESOURCES

Use a Bible dictionary by looking up the word, person, or item that you are studying. Sometimes a Bible dictionary will refer you to related selections.

Write in the margin two things a Bible dictionary says about angels.

If you know a word in a verse, but can't find the verse, look up the word in a *Bible concordance*. You can find other passages that relate to that word through a Bible concordance or a *topical Bible*.

In the margin list references for five verses that contain the word *grace*.

Look at a *Bible atlas* and a map of the world today. Abraham came from the city of Ur on the Euphrates River. What country now occupies that land?

Day 5
Ready to Get Started?

Congratulations! You've stuck with your commitment to learn how to study the Bible by getting to day 5! What struggles did you face this week that made it hard to stay faithful to your commitment? List them in the margin.

Pause and thank God for guiding you through this first week of study. Ask for God's wisdom and guidance as you work on today's study.

In the next five weeks, you'll learn specific techniques for studying and understanding the Bible. This week you've looked at the tools to make that study effective. Let's see if you understand which tools can help you with specific studies.

Which of the these tools would you use to find the following information (you might use more than one study resource):

a. modern translations
b. paraphrased translations
c. concordance
d. Bible dictionary
e. topical Bible
f. Bible atlas
g. Bible commentary
h. Bible encyclopedia

_____ Who was Barak?
_____ What is the meaning of Peter's dream in *Acts 10:9-18*?
_____ What does the Bible say about divorce?
_____ How would *1 Corinthians 8:2* read in modern-day language?
_____ How many times is God mentioned in the book of Esther?
_____ What countries took the Israelites into captivity?
_____ Through what modern-day countries did Paul take his first missionary journey?
_____ What does *1 Thessalonians 5:24* mean?
_____ Why did the Jews in Jesus' day hate the Samaritans?
_____ Where does a donkey speak in the Bible?

A STUDENT'S GUIDE TO STUDYING THE BIBLE

If you have some of these Bible tools available, try to find answers to the questions that most intrigued you.

Before you finish today, write down questions you have about the Bible, about Bible passages you have read and don't understand, or about people in the Bible you want to study. Write your questions here:

1. _____
2. _____
3. _____
4. _____

Over the next five weeks you will look at many verses and gain new insight. Once you are through with this study, you will continue on your own. Take a few minutes to identify Bible study topics and books that you might like to study in the future. Check all that interest you.

- ❏ sin
- ❏ death
- ❏ assurance of salvation
- ❏ the prayers of Jesus
- ❏ the prophecies about Jesus' life and death
- ❏ Jonathan and David's relationship

- ❏ judgment
- ❏ peace
- ❏ holiness
- ❏ the promises of Jesus
- ❏ the Book of John
- ❏ the Book of Ruth
- ❏ Joseph's story
- ❏ Noah's story

Add your own . . .

_____
_____

Write this week's Scripture memory passage and Scripture reference in the margin before you end today's session with prayer.

---

[1] Scripture quotations identified KJV are from the *King James Version*.
[2] Scripture quotations marked RSV are from the *Revised Standard Version of the Bible*, copyrighted 1946, 1952, © 1971, 1973.
[3] Scripture quotations marked GNB are from the *Good News Bible*, the Bible in Today's English Version. Old Testament: Copyright © American Bible Society 1966, 1971, 1976. Used by permission.
[4] Scripture quotations marked NASB are from the NEW AMERICAN STANDARD BIBLE.
© Copyright The Lockman Foundation, 1960, 1962, 1963, 1968, 1971, 1972, 1973, 1975, 1977, 1995. Used by permission.
[5] Scripture quotations marked CEV are from the *Contemporary English Version*, Copyright © American Bible Society 1991, 1992. Used by permission.
[6] Scripture quotations marked TLB are from *The Living Bible*. Copyright © Tyndale House Publishers. Wheaton, Illinois, 1971. Used by permission.
[7] Scripture quotations identified as *The Message* are from *The Message*. Copyright © 1993, 1994, 1995. Used by permission of NavPress Publishing Group.
[8] From the *Williams New Testament, The New Testament in the Language of the People*, by Charles B. Williams. Copyright © 1937, 1966, 1986 by Holman Bible Publishers. Used by permission.

Week 2
One Bible Study Prerequisite

This week you will:
- review the relationship needed to develop a desire to study the Bible;
- discover which type of Bible study student you are;
- evaluate the attitude needed to be an effective Bible student;
- learn how God's gift guides you in understanding the Bible;
- discover ways to discipline yourself in Bible study.

This Week's Bible Study Tip
Check which statements best express your feelings.
- 1. I listen to music while I study.
- 2. I learn best from pictures or visuals.
- 3. I prefer to complete a project on my own.
- 4. Talking about what I need to learn helps me understand.
- 5. When others talk, I see images in my mind.
- 6. I prefer to figure out things for myself.

If you checked numbers 1 and 4, you learn best by hearing. Enlist a friend to work with you on this study. Talk about each day's material. Challenge one another to do the memory work and complete the daily study.

If you checked numbers 2 and 5, you learn best by seeing. When this study guide asks you to write down your thoughts, draw yours. Use doodles and stick-figure art with cartoon-type blurbs to get across your ideas.

If you checked number 3 and 6, you learn best by doing. Be careful not to skim over the information. Look for ways to get involved with the material. For example, design your own Bible study response questions.

This Week's Scripture Memory Passage
The man without the Spirit does not accept the things that come from the Spirit of God, for they are foolishness to him, and he cannot understand them, because they are spiritually discerned (1 Cor. 2:14).

This Week's Lessons
Day 1: A Spiritual Hunger to Be in God's Family
Day 2: A Spiritual Hunger to Learn About God
Day 3: A Spiritual Hunger that Begins With a Teachable Attitude
Day 4: A Spiritual Hunger that Depends on the Holy Spirit
Day 5: A Spiritual Hunger that Develops Discipline

A STUDENT'S GUIDE TO STUDYING THE BIBLE

Day 1
A Spiritual Hunger to Be in God's Family

Read and mark *1 Corinthians 2:14* **in your Bible. Use your Scripture memory card to begin memorizing** *1 Corinthians 2:14.*

Last week you learned this study is composed of five subject areas. You also saw how each subject area would be represented by one of the fingers on the diagram of your hand.

What is the first area that goes on the thumb?
One Bible Study P __ __ __ __ __ __ __ __ __ __ __ __

Write a brief definition of prerequisite. _____
_____
_____

A prerequisite is something that is required or essential before you can go any further. What one prerequisite is necessary for Bible study? (HINT: Look at today's title.)
A S __ __ __ __ __ __ __ __   H __ __ __ __ __

Write "One Prerequisite: A Spiritual Hunger" on the thumb of the hand you drew on the inside cover of this book.

If you desire interesting, effective Bible study, you must have a spiritual hunger for God's Word. This week you will study how to develop and keep a hunger for knowing more about God's Word. Today's study is about the most important relationship you will ever experience.

Check all the relationships that are important to you.
❑ strong family ties with parents
❑ good relationship with brother(s) and/or sister(s)
❑ healthy relationships with friends from church
❑ healthy relationships with friends at school
❑ friendships with those on your team (or club)

ONE BIBLE STUDY PREREQUISITE

- ❏ a positive relationship with a favorite teacher
- ❏ a pleasant relationship with a favorite coach
- ❏ a girlfriend or boyfriend relationship
- ❏ a role model to follow
- ❏ a personal experience with Jesus Christ

Circle the relationship that will cause you to be spiritually hungry for God's Word.

You are exactly right if you circled the last option. You won't hunger to know about God or want to understand the truths in God's Word until you are part of God's family. God brings you into His family when you accept Jesus Christ as your personal Savior. Some students think you can join God's family in other ways. Maybe you've had these same thoughts.

Write a response to the following statements that you've heard or said.
"I don't do anything really bad." _____
_____
"I go to church and several Bible studies." _____
_____
"I'm nice to everyone." _____
_____
"My parents are Christians; I was raised in the church." _____
_____

Read *Titus 3:4-5* in your Bible. Compare it to the translation below. How does a person establish a relationship with God?

When the kindness and love of God our Savior was revealed, he saved us. It was not because of any good deeds that we ourselves had done, but because of his own mercy. . . . (TEV).[1]

A relationship with God is based on God's love which He showed us through Jesus Christ. You can't earn a trip to heaven by your own efforts. How does a person accept God's love and join God's family? Read *John 1:12* and summarize it in the margin.

You become a child of God, a part of God's family, by believing in Jesus Christ as your personal Lord and Savior. God gives eternal life as a gift to those who trust Jesus. A child of God, a Christian, knows this, but a non-Christian has trouble understanding. How do the words of God appear to someone outside God's family according to Paul in *1 Corinthians 2:14*?

Earthly families have a similar situation. They have inside jokes and stories that those outside the family don't understand.

> **A relationship with God is based on God's love which He showed us through Jesus Christ.**

A STUDENT'S GUIDE TO STUDYING THE BIBLE

Write down a couple of your family's inside jokes, sayings or traditions. (This could include anything from a nickname to a funny line from a family joke.) _____
_____
_____
_____
_____

Why is the Bible clear to a member of God's family? Read *John 14:26* to complete this sentence: The Holy Spirit _____ God's truths.

When you become a member of God's family, God gives you the Holy Spirit to teach you the inside, family information. The person who doesn't have the Holy Spirit living in them, doesn't understand the Scripture. Even the promises and commandments of the Bible appear puzzling and unrealistic.

Why do you want to study the Bible? _____
_____
_____

Why do you want to understand what you study? _____
_____
_____

How do you expect your life to be changed by what you read? _____
_____
_____

When you hunger to know more about God, He will show you the way. Memorizing Scripture supports your study. Memorizing is easy when you:
• Have a positive attitude.
• Work at it each day.
• Review regularly.

The Scripture memory passage cards on pages 109-110 in this book contain each week's Scripture memory passage. Cut the cards apart. Locate the *1 Corinthians 2:14* Scripture memory card and begin to memorize today.

> The person who doesn't have the Holy Spirit living in them, doesn't understand the Scripture. Even the promises and commandments of the Bible appear puzzling and unrealistic.

ONE BIBLE STUDY PREREQUISITE

Day 2
A Spiritual Hunger to Learn About God

Being in God's family makes you want to learn more about God. God's Word provides a great way to know God better.

Yesterday you studied an important relationship that makes you spiritually hungry to understand the teachings of the Bible. Describe that basic relationship here:
_____
_____

Did you remember that you need a personal relationship with Jesus Christ so that you can be a member of God's family? Family members understand one another better than those outside the family.

Today you will study a second reason why you develop a spiritual hunger. Being in God's family makes you want to learn more about God. God's Word provides a great way to know God better.

Compare this idea to wanting to learn to play tennis. Which person in the following situations really wants to learn how to play tennis?
❑ The one who buys a tennis racket, books about playing tennis, and a neat tennis outfit.
❑ The one who takes tennis in gym class, but only plays at school.
❑ The one who studies the subject thoroughly, then practices, practices, and practices.
❑ The one who asks for tips from tennis pros.

Obviously, the one who studies and practices tennis is most likely to master the sport. Others show an interest in the game, but fail to do the work required.
   Three types of people say they want to study the Bible.
Bible Student Number One—This student studies the Bible for the wrong reasons.

What are some superficial reasons for studying God's Word? Check those you've experienced. Be honest. This is between you and God.
❑ curious about religion
❑ to be a part of a popular Bible study group
❑ to be with friends

25

- ❏ everyone expects you to participate
- ❏ to please your youth minister
- ❏ to feel more spiritual
- ❏ to make you a better person
- ❏ because it's required to go on a mission trip
- ❏ because there's nothing else to do
- ❏ (add your own idea) _____

Bible Student Number Two—This Bible student is a Bible-student-wannabe. This student says he wants to study the Bible, but various circumstances tempt this person away from regular Bible study.

Check the distractions that keep you from being a consistent, serious Bible student.
- ❏ doing fun things with friends
- ❏ working at a job that takes a lot of time
- ❏ having lots of homework
- ❏ working on a major project for school
- ❏ being involved in after-school activities
- ❏ having numerous activities at church
- ❏ being too tired
- ❏ being sick or recovering from an accident
- ❏ letting friends interfere
- ❏ running errands for your family

Bible Student Number Three—This Bible student eagerly overcomes obstacles in order to learn and apply the teachings of the Bible to life. *Psalm 1:2* describes this person.

Read *Psalm 1:2* and then fill in the blanks.
His _____ is in the _____ _____ _____ _____, and on his law he _____ _____ and _____.

This student wants to know and obey God. He takes time to study God's Word. This student seeks to live by the principles of the Scriptures. He measures his actions day and night by God's standards, not by what other people think.

Last week your Scripture memory passage was *Psalm 19:7-8*. Read *Psalm 19:7-14*. Summarize *verses 7-9* by stating how the writer feels about the different parts of God's Word. _____
_____
_____

ONE BIBLE STUDY PREREQUISITE

Summarize the psalmist's feelings about God's Words in *verse 10.* ____
_____
_____

God's Word warns of temptations, offers cleansing in your heart and mind, and gives victory over deceitful, enslaving sins.

Mark in your Bible the blessing of *Psalm 19:13.*

What are your goals for Bible study? What needs do you have that Bible study can meet? What benefits do you hope to receive as you become a better student of God's Word? List positive, healthy reasons to study God's Word. (HINT: Use some of the ideas of the psalmist.)

- _____
- _____
- _____
- _____

Review this week's Scripture memory passage. End today's study with prayer. Ask God to make you eager to study His Word. Ask God to help you deal with distractions that might keep you from studying the Bible.

Day 3
A Spiritual Hunger That Begins with A Teachable Attitude

This week you are studying the "One Prerequisite" needed to study God's Word. That prerequisite is a spiritual hunger to know God's Word. In days 1 and 2 you looked at two requirements for a spiritual hunger.

- The vital relationship needed is _____.
- The desire needed is _____.

Did you write something like "being a member of God's family" and "having the desire to learn"? If so, you are right. Today you will look at another requirement—a teachable attitude.

Read *Psalm 119:24, 33-40, 105, 108.*

This psalm talks about being eager to know God's Word and being willing to respond to God's Word.

List the attitudes and actions mentioned in these verses that indicate the writer's teachable attitude.
Verse 24: _____

Verses 33-40: _____

Verse 105: _____

Verse 108: _____

Psalm 119 contains many verses that show a teachable attitude. The verses you read here represent just a few. In *Psalm 119:24* the psalmist showed his delight in the Word of God. It was his counselor.

How does the Bible "counsel" someone who studies it? _____
_____
_____

Psalm 119:33-40 is a prayer for understanding. The words in *Psalm 119:105* show that the psalmist used God's Word as a guide for living.

How does the Bible guide a person's life? _____
_____
_____

Psalm 119:108 indicates an openness, obedience, and a willingness to learn. The psalmist saw that God's words provided a solution to his problems.

Think of an experience when your parents, a teacher, or someone else tried to teach you something you didn't want to learn. Write down the feelings you had about the experience. _____
_____
_____

ONE BIBLE STUDY PREREQUISITE

Now, write down the feelings you had at a time when you wanted to learn something. _____
_____
_____

Having a teachable attitude begins with your feelings. You won't learn if you don't want to learn. God shows His truths and commandments to those who are teachable. Those who don't want to learn receive no spiritual understanding.

Read *John 15:14-15*, and then answer the following questions.
Who are Jesus' friends? _____
_____

What did Jesus promise to do for His friends? _____

> **God shows His truths and commandments to those who are teachable. Those who don't want to learn receive no spiritual understanding.**

The friends of Jesus are those who are teachable and obedient. Jesus wants to teach His friends everything He learned from His Father. As a teachable friend, you can learn a lot about God's message.

Think of a time when you and your friends learned something together. How did learning with a friend increase your desire to learn? _____
_____

Certain negative factors affect a person's teachable attitude. In *Mark 4:1-20*, Jesus used a parable to identify three negative factors.

Read *Mark 4:1-20* to identify these factors.
Verse 15—Seeds thrown on the hard, dirt path don't sprout. This is like the learner who . . . _____
_____

Verses 16-17—Seeds thrown on rocky soil sprout quickly, but don't have a good root system. This is like the learner who . . . _____
_____

Verses 18-19—Seeds thrown in the thorny soil take root, but are choked out by the thorns and weeds. This is like the learner who . . . _____
_____

Some respond to God's Word like seeds sown beside the road in hard soil. Their minds are closed to God's truths. Some respond in a superficial way. They get excited about God's Word, but when the newness wears off or troubles come, they lose interest. Others study God's Word only in the good times. When instant learning doesn't occur, or worries become too great, they quit.

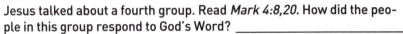

A STUDENT'S GUIDE TO STUDYING THE BIBLE

Jesus talked about a fourth group. Read *Mark 4:8,20*. How did the people in this group respond to God's Word? _____

When you allow God to teach you, exciting things happen. The fact that you are doing this study shows that you want to be in the growth group. These believers welcome the Word of God like rich soil welcomes seed. This soil will produce an abundant crop.

Even though you want to be like the fourth seed in Jesus' example, you may still struggle with rocky areas or worries in your life.

List areas or worries that might destroy your teachable attitude:
_____
_____

> When you allow God to teach you, exciting things happen. The fact that you are doing this study shows that you want to be in the growth group.

Jesus understands your struggles because He experienced these same struggles Himself. He promises to help you. Imagine that!

What does *Hebrews 4:16* say you need to do to get the help you need? ___
_____

Pray to God. Claim His promise of help. Pray about your struggles today.

Day 4
A Spiritual Hunger That Depends on the Holy Spirit

Agree or disagree with the following statements:
agree/disagree 1. The Bible is hard to understand because it contains confusing words and difficult ideas.
agree/disagree 2. The Bible is difficult to understand because I am a student, too young to comprehend.

ONE BIBLE STUDY PREREQUISITE

agree/disagree 3. I know God wants me to understand the message of the Bible.
agree/disagree 4. I can figure out the Bible by myself.

Some youth are defeated before they ever get started in Bible study. They think the Bible is too difficult to read and understand. Other youth are more enthusiastic. They believe God speaks clearly to them as they study the Bible. What makes the difference?

The key is the Holy Spirit. Depending on the Holy Spirit is the fourth ingredient in responding to the One Prerequisite of spiritual hunger. The Holy Spirit comes to a Christian at the time that person accepts Jesus Christ as their personal Savior. This personal Teacher makes the Bible come alive. The Holy Spirit shows you how to apply biblical teachings to life.

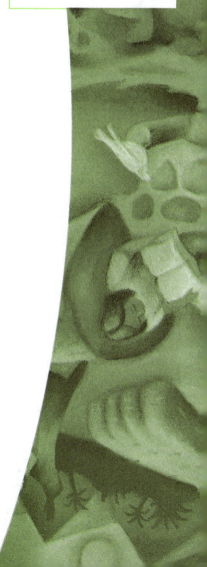

The Holy Spirit comes to a Christian at the time that person accepts Jesus Christ as their personal Savior. This personal Teacher makes the Bible come alive.

Read *John 16:13-15.* Name one specific task of the Holy Spirit. _____
_____
_____

How can the Holy Spirit guide you? _____
_____
_____

Where do you need the most help in Bible study? Check all that apply.
❑ understanding words   ❑ putting stories together
❑ making stories relevant   ❑ making the Bible personal
❑ staying interested   ❑ interpreting hard verses
❑ (add your own needs) _____

God Himself in the person of the Holy Spirit dwells in you and is with you each time you open your Bible to study. He is your personal guide. He assists you in Bible study.

How are you doing with this week's Scripture memory passage? Write *1 Corinthians 2:14* here without looking at your Scripture memory passage card or your Bible. _____
_____
_____
_____
_____
_____
_____

This verse from *1 Corinthians* is part of a passage that describes other things about the Holy Spirit's role as a teacher.

A STUDENT'S GUIDE TO STUDYING THE BIBLE

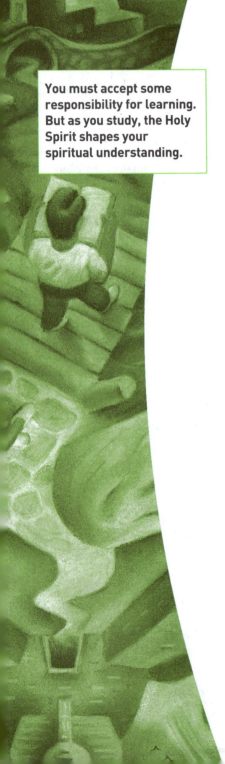

Read *1 Corinthians 2:10-14*. List why the Holy Spirit is the ideal Teacher of God's truths.

• _____
_____
• _____
_____

> You must accept some responsibility for learning. But as you study, the Holy Spirit shapes your spiritual understanding.

The Holy Spirit knows the deep truths of God. The Holy Spirit won't provide biblical information that you can look up in a Bible dictionary or read in a commentary. You must accept some responsibility for learning. But as you study, the Holy Spirit shapes your spiritual understanding.

From the moment you became a Christian, the Holy Spirit has been teaching and guiding you.

Think of a time when the Holy Spirit helped you understand something about God. Describe that experience here.

The Holy Spirit helped me to understand. . . _____
_____
_____

Once I was frustrated because I couldn't do something I thought God wanted me to do. I really believed God called me to do this job. One day I was reading the Bible, and I found an answer in *1 Thessalonians 5:24*. Loosely translated it says: When God calls you to a task, He will do it through you. Shortly afterwards the job was finished! Here is what the Holy Spirit can do for you.
- The Holy Spirit makes you spiritually receptive.
- The Holy Spirit sharpens your mind to figure out Bible principles.
- The Holy Spirit clarifies Bible passages.
- The Holy Spirit makes you wise about what the Bible says.
- The Holy Spirit helps you apply Bible teachings to your life.
- The Holy Spirit is your ultimate Teacher.

While the Holy Spirit is your ultimate, final Teacher, He uses other resources. Check the resources that are available to help you.
- ❑ an adult you respect
- ❑ the Internet
- ❑ a friend who studies the Bible with you
- ❑ Christian music
- ❑ Bible studies on CD ROMs
- ❑ commentaries, Bible dictionaries, lesson books
- ❑ group Bible studies with Christian friends
- ❑ (write your own ideas) _____
_____

ONE BIBLE STUDY PREREQUISITE

Perhaps you are wondering how you can get in touch with the Holy Spirit in Bible study.
- Expect to meet the Holy Spirit in Bible study. Be positive and excited.
- Begin Bible study with a prayer for guidance. Ask the Spirit to open your mind and heart.
- Share your questions about the Bible with others who are studying the Bible. Ask the Holy Spirit to speak through them.
- As you read, don't get in a hurry. Give the Spirit time to help you remember related experiences and events.
- Be consistent. If you only talked to a friend once a year, you wouldn't feel like close friends. But if you talk daily, your friendship is deeper. You become more sensitive to the Spirit when you communicate every day.

In the margin write a prayer asking for the Holy Spirit's guidance.

Day 5
A Spiritual Hunger That Develops Discipline

What has been the subject or theme for this week? (HINT: You wrote it on the thumb of your hand in the front of this book.)

One Bible Study P__ __ __ __ __ __ __ __ __ __
A serious Bible student must have a
S__ __ __ __ __ __ __ __ __   H__ __ __ __ __ __

The one prerequisite needed for the serious student of the Bible is to have a spiritual hunger for the Word of God. Every day you've studied what it takes to create and to keep that spiritual hunger.

A STUDENT'S GUIDE TO STUDYING THE BIBLE

First, you need a vital _____ with God through Jesus Christ.
Next, you need a spiritual hunger to _____ about God.
Third, you need a _____ attitude.

Today you will see how discipline in your study habits keeps you spiritually hungry for God's Word.

Indicate if you agree or disagree with the following statements.
agree/disagree 1. Professional athletes learn best by watching videos of their sport.
agree/disagree 2. Anyone can pick up an instrument and learn to play it within a few hours.
agree/disagree 3. Practice makes perfect.
agree/disagree 4. No pain, no gain.
agree/disagree 5. Christians can best learn God's truths, commands, and promises by letting the Holy Spirit do the work.

Athletes, musicians, writers, doctors, engineers, computer programmers, actresses—almost any profession—don't become "over-night sensations" without a lot of practice. Many jobs require a person to spend hours doing the same activity over and over. Other professions allow little room for error so the person must be well-trained and highly skilled. No one gets that training or that skill without discipline and hard work. The same is true for the Bible student. It takes discipline to stick with Bible study. Check out Paul's advice to Timothy about discipline.

Read *2 Timothy 2:15* in several Bible translations. Read in the margin two translations that you may not have.

What did Paul urge Timothy to do? _____
_____

What kind of discipline did Timothy need to achieve what Paul asked?
_____
_____

How do Paul's words apply to you? _____
_____
_____

Paul urged Timothy to work hard and make the effort to learn. All Christians must work hard to develop the ability to interpret and apply God's Word to their lives. What does it mean for a Christian to be disciplined in order to understand the Bible?

WARNING!! Just because the Holy Spirit helps you, doesn't mean you have all the answers. You hurt God and others when you say something like, "The Holy Spirit gave me this solution, and that's the way it is!" Replace pride and arrogance with humility. Share what you believe God teaches you through the Holy Spirit and the Bible, but don't push your ideas on others. Instead, share your ideas with kindness.

Concentrate on doing your best for God, work you won't be ashamed of, laying out the truth plain and simple (The Message, by Eugene Peterson).²

Do your best to win God's approval as a worker who doesn't need to be ashamed and who teaches only the true message (CEV).³

Check those disciplines you need to be a serious Bible student.
- ❏ learn new words
- ❏ seek to understand the culture of the Bible
- ❏ examine the facts surrounding the passage you are studying
- ❏ learn about the customs of the people
- ❏ be open to new thoughts about God, Jesus and the Holy Spirit
- ❏ keep a good attitude
- ❏ find time for Bible study
- ❏ stay focused while studying
- ❏ read the Bible with interest and a desire to learn
- ❏ learn about resources that can help you study
- ❏ pray about your Bible study
- ❏ ask a friend to keep you accountable for consistent Bible study
- ❏ see Bible study as an adventure
- ❏ practice listening to God and what He wants you to learn
- ❏ expect new ideas and insights

OK. Let's review this week of study.

FIRST, say aloud the Scripture memory passage for this week.
NEXT, review the necessary elements to create and keep a spiritual hunger for God's Word. There are five actions or attitudes that you need to develop a spiritual hunger for the Word of God. (I've given you the first.) I need to . . .
1. develop a personal relationship with God through Jesus Christ. _____
2. _____
3. _____
4. _____
5. _____

Over the next four weeks you will develop and practice the skills needed for interpreting and applying God's Word. In your prayer today state your commitment to God and ask for discipline in your Bible study.

---

[1] This quotation is from the *Good News Bible*, the Bible in Today's English Version. Old Testament: Copyright © American Bible Society 1976; New Testament: Copyright © American Bible Society 1966, 1971, 1976. Used by permission.
[2] Scripture quotations identified as *The Message* are from *The Message*. Copyright © 1993, 1994, 1995. Used by permission of NavPress Publishing Group.
[3] Scripture quotations marked CEV are from the *Contemporary English Version*, Copyright © American Bible Society 1991, 1992. Used by permission.

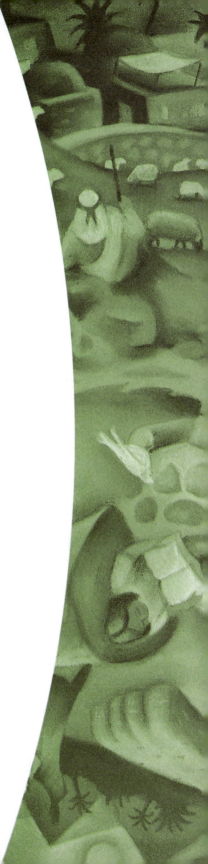

This Week's Scripture Memory Passage
Humble yourselves, therefore, under God's mighty hand, that he may lift you up in due time. Cast all your anxiety on him because he cares for you (1 Pet. 5:6-7).

This Week's Lessons
Day 1: Interpret the Bible Correctly, Part 1
Day 2: Interpret the Bible Correctly, Part 2
Day 3: Interpret the Bible Correctly, Part 3
Day 4: Apply the Bible Wisely, Part 1
Day 5: Apply the Bible Wisely, Part 2

Week 3
Two Rules to Guide Bible Study

This week you will:
- learn five guidelines for interpreting the Bible correctly;
- learn five guidelines for applying the Bible wisely to your life;
- practice these guidelines through several examples of Scripture.

THIS WEEK'S BIBLE STUDY TIP

Place each week's Scripture memory card where you will see it during the day. For example, you might place it on a mirror. Or, attach it to your calendar. If you drive, stick it in the car where you can review the Scripture memory passage at traffic lights or when you are waiting on someone. Make additional copies of the Scripture memory passage to stick around your environment—on the table where you eat meals, in the front of a notebook, next to the screen of your computer. The more places you place each week's Scripture memory passage, the more likely you are to work on it and remember it.

Keep in mind that the purpose of memorizing is to make the Bible something that becomes a part of your world. You will be surprised how frequently you recall these verses when you don't have a Bible available to look them up.

TWO RULES TO GUIDE BIBLE STUDY

Day 1
Interpret the Bible Correctly, Part 1

Read and mark *1 Peter 5:6-7* in your Bible. Use your Scripture memory card to begin memorizing these verses.

This week offers two rules to guide your Bible study. The rules are Interpret the Bible Correctly and Apply the Bible Wisely. Each rule has five guidelines. To make it easier to remember the five guidelines for each rule use two acrostics. For rule 1 (Interpret the Bible Correctly), use the first five letters of *interpret*.

On the hand you drew in the front of this book, write "Two Rules to Guide Bible Study" on the index finger.

RULE 1—INTERPRET THE BIBLE CORRECTLY

I dentify the type of writing.
N ote the context.
T rust the Bible to interpret itself.
E xamine the writer's meaning.
R emember the limits of revelation.

For the second rule (Apply the Bible Wisely), use the word *apply* to remember the main guidelines.

RULE 2—APPLY THE BIBLE WISELY.

A sk what the verse means.
P ractice the Bible as a book of standards.
P lug in the promises carefully.
L earn about the culture.
Y ou must understand the technique of overstatement.

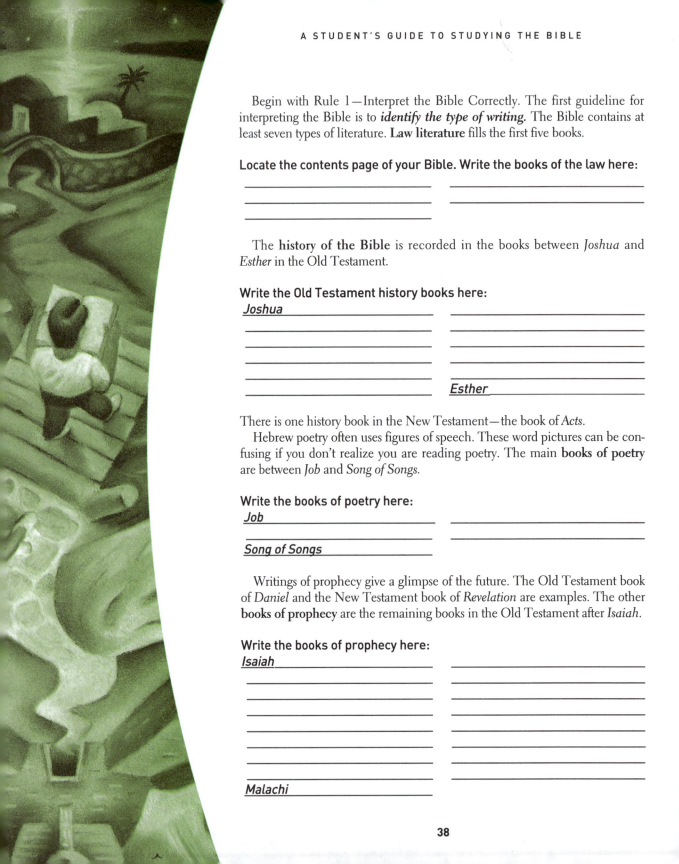

A STUDENT'S GUIDE TO STUDYING THE BIBLE

Begin with Rule 1—Interpret the Bible Correctly. The first guideline for interpreting the Bible is to *identify the type of writing*. The Bible contains at least seven types of literature. **Law literature** fills the first five books.

Locate the contents page of your Bible. Write the books of the law here:

_____   _____
_____   _____
_____

The **history of the Bible** is recorded in the books between *Joshua* and *Esther* in the Old Testament.

Write the Old Testament history books here:
*Joshua*_____   _____
_____   _____
_____   _____
_____   _____
_____   *Esther*_____

There is one history book in the New Testament—the book of *Acts*.

Hebrew poetry often uses figures of speech. These word pictures can be confusing if you don't realize you are reading poetry. The main **books of poetry** are between *Job* and *Song of Songs*.

Write the books of poetry here:
*Job*_____   _____
_____   _____
*Song of Songs*_____

Writings of prophecy give a glimpse of the future. The Old Testament book of *Daniel* and the New Testament book of *Revelation* are examples. The other **books of prophecy** are the remaining books in the Old Testament after *Isaiah*.

Write the books of prophecy here:
*Isaiah*_____   _____
_____   _____
_____   _____
_____   _____
_____   _____
_____   _____
*Malachi*_____

TWO RULES TO GUIDE BIBLE STUDY

Narrative writings relate events that describe what God has done in history. The books of **narrative biography** about Jesus are *Matthew, Mark, Luke,* and *John*. Other books of narrative writings are *Genesis* and *Exodus* in the Old Testament and *Acts* in the New Testament.

The New Testament also has **letters** from Paul, Peter, John, and others. These letters teach God's message to young Christians. Sometimes these books are called **epistles.** Scholars believe Paul wrote many of the New Testament letters beginning with *Romans* and ending with *Philemon*.

List Paul's letters here:
Romans _____ _____
_____ _____
_____ _____
_____ _____
_____ _____
Philemon _____

Some books of the Bible contain several kinds of writing. *Isaiah* for example, has poetry, prophecy, and narrative sections. Most books fit into one type of literature, even though a book contains elements of other kinds of writing.

Write the major types of biblical literature here:
L_____, H_____, P_____, P_____, N_____ (also called Biography), and L_____ (also called epistles).

Let's use this information to identify the type of literature in the following Scripture. Be careful. Don't assume that a verse is one type just because the book is listed under that type of literature.

Read *Isaiah 1:15-16.* What type of literature is this? _____
_____

Most Bible translations see this writing as poetry. The people's prayers offended God because the people had turned against God. Under God's leadership, Isaiah told the people to wash and make themselves clean. He didn't mean a bath and a bar of soap would remove the guilt of sin. This is a figure of speech.

Read *Acts 3:1-7.* What type of literature is this? _____
_____

This narrative describes Peter's healing of a man who was born crippled. In narrative writing, simply look at the details.

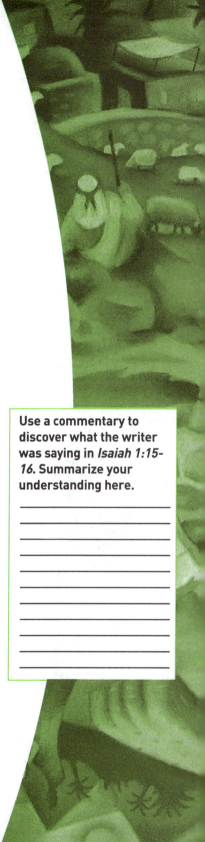

Use a commentary to discover what the writer was saying in *Isaiah 1:15-16.* Summarize your understanding here.
_____
_____
_____
_____
_____
_____
_____
_____
_____
_____
_____
_____

A STUDENT'S GUIDE TO STUDYING THE BIBLE

Read *Colossians 4:2-3.* What type of literature is this? _____

In this letter from Paul to the Colossian church Paul asked the people to pray for his work. Decide what figure of speech is used in *verse* 3 and look in a commentary to see what it means.

Day 2
Interpret the Bible Correctly, Part 2

I dentify the type of writing.
N ote the context.
T rust the Bible to interpret itself.
E xamine the writer's meaning.
R emember the limits of revelation.

Yesterday you learned that the first guideline in interpreting a Scripture passage is to *identify the type of writing.* You learned that there are many types of literature within the Bible. Some books of the Bible contain several types of literature.

A second guideline in interpreting the Bible correctly is to **note the context.** Context refers to two separate things.
1. Context involves the biblical section where the verse or passage appears. Biblical context includes the verses around a verse.
2. Context also involves the wider context of an entire book. You may need to know why the book was written and to whom, even the culture.

To understand the importance of the biblical context, read *Matthew 6:6.*

Where does it sound like Jesus meant was the only place to pray? _____
_____

TWO RULES TO GUIDE BIBLE STUDY

Now read *Matthew 6:1-7* (the verses surrounding *v. 6*). After reading *Matthew 6:6* in context, what did Jesus emphasize? _____
_____

Context shows that Jesus emphasized the motive behind the prayer. Prayer focuses on sincere communication with God, rather than impressing others with churchy-sounding words.

The broader context of a Bible passage includes knowledge of biblical social customs, history, or geography. Knowing the circumstances of the writer can make a verse more clear. You can discover the broader context of social and cultural issues by using a Bible commentary and a Bible dictionary. Let's test this idea of a broader context.

Read Paul's joy-filled words in *Philippians 4:4*. Then look at *Philippians 1:12-13* to discover where Paul was and the conditions under which he was living.

Considering Paul's situation, what makes Paul's words of exclamation in *Philippians 4:4* so unique? _____
_____

> Are you working on this week's Scripture memory passage *1 Peter 5:6-7?* See how you're doing by filling in the missing words.
>
> _____ *yourselves, therefore,* under _____ *mighty* _____ , *that he may* _____ _____ _____ *in due time.* _____ *all your* _____ *on him because he* _____ *for you* (1 Pet. 5:6-7).

Paul wrote these words of joy while under house arrest. *Acts 28:16,30* explains that Paul was likely chained to a guard and confined to his house. If Paul could be joyful in that situation, the strength of God must be great! The context of Paul's situation makes the verse even more meaningful.

The third technique to interpret the Bible is to ***trust the Bible to interpret itself.*** Many Bible passages are difficult to understand. Often a clearer passage in the Bible can explain a difficult passage. Many biblical topics appear in more than one passage. Topics discussed briefly in one section may be more fully presented in another. Use the more detailed passage to understand the smaller, related verses. For example, if you want to study the resurrection of Christ look in *1 Corinthians 15*. *Hebrews 11* explains the nature of faith.

Practice using the Bible to interpret the Bible.

Read *Matthew 21:22*. In the space below write a statement expressing what this verse says. _____
_____
_____

Some people may think this passage means a person can get anything they want from God if they just have enough faith. If so, hooray! So where do you want your new car parked? Go ahead and mark Friday night as the BIG DATE you've been waiting for! Clean out your room and create some space for the year's worth of top 40 CDs you're about to receive!

A STUDENT'S GUIDE TO STUDYING THE BIBLE

Hang on! Let's see how other Bible verses explain this one particular verse. Read *John 14:13; James 4:3;* and *1 John 5:14-15*. How do these verses change your original interpretation of *Matthew 21:22*? _____
_____
_____
_____

John 14:13 affirms the truth that faith alone does not guarantee answered prayer, especially those prayers that go against God's will. *James 4:3* explains that God will not answer prayer if your motive is selfish. *First John 5:14-15* indicates how God's will is the crucial factor in receiving an answer to prayer. These passages on prayer show that many factors determine how prayers are answered. To understand what the Bible teaches on a subject like prayer, consider the entire Bible. Looking only at one passage may cause an incorrect interpretation. Use the Bible to interpret itself.

Lets review: There are two rules to guide Bible study.

Rule 1 is Interpret the _____ _____.

You have studied three of the five ways to interpret the Bible. The first letter of each guideline should help you remember.

I_____.
N_____.
T_____.
E xamine the writer's meaning.
R emember the limits of revelation.

Write this week's Scripture memory passage in the margin.

42

Day 3
Interpret the Bible Correctly, Part 3

I dentify the type of writing.
N ote the context.
T rust the Bible to interpret itself.
E xamine the writer's meaning.
R emember the limits of revelation.

Today you will study the last two guidelines for interpreting the Bible correctly. The fourth guideline is to *examine the writer's meaning*. Two keys help you examine the meaning of a passage.

Key 1— Determine the obvious meaning of a passage by asking this question, "What was the writer or speaker trying to say?"

Read *Matthew 7:12* and state in your own words what Jesus meant.
_____
_____

Passages like this are not difficult to understand.

Key 2— Understand figures of speech or word pictures.

Read *Psalm 91:4* and write down how God is described.
_____
_____

If you interpret this verse based on the words, you would say God has feathers and wings. The psalm actually means that God's love and protection is like a hen covering her chicks with feathers and wings.

How can you discover the meaning of verses like these? A Bible commen-

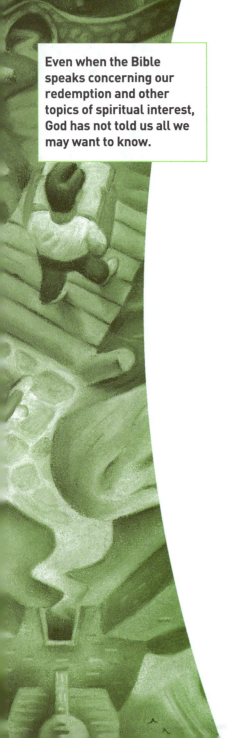

tary helps. You also can talk to your pastor or another experienced Bible student (adult or friend). Read the passages on this chart. Then write in the left column what you think the writer or speaker meant. Use a commentary.

MEANING	APPLICATIONS
Psalm 119:105	
_____	_____
_____	_____
John 6:35	
_____	_____
_____	_____
Matthew 7:3-4	
_____	_____
_____	_____

While a passage may have one meaning, it can be applied in different ways. Based on your understanding of these passages, how would you apply these verses to your life? Write your application ideas in the right column. (For example, for *Ps. 119:105* you might write *I can use the Bible to guide my life.*)

The final guideline for interpreting the Bible is to **remember the limits of revelation.** The Bible speaks on many subjects, but it does not contain information on every subject. Sometimes a Bible student draws more from the Bible than God intended. To avoid misinterpretation consider these points:

- The Bible's purpose is to outline God's plan of redemption through Christ.
- While the Bible certainly speaks to many issues such as science and medicine, it is not intended to be a complete textbook on those subjects.
- Even when the Bible speaks concerning our redemption and other topics of spiritual interest, God has not told us all we may want to know.
- The words of the Bible are inspirationally complete. We must be content with this information and not try to go beyond what it says.

Here's an example of the limitations of the Bible—

Scripture promises that Jesus Christ will return again. *Titus 2:11-13* and *1 Thessalonians 4:13-18* gloriously describe this event. However, the Bible doesn't give the exact time of Jesus' return. Even Jesus didn't know the time of His return.

Read *Mark 13:32-37*. What did Jesus want us to know about His return?
1. _____
2. _____

Jesus gave assurance of His return, and he wanted us to be ready.

TWO RULES TO GUIDE BIBLE STUDY

What are some predictions others have made about Jesus' return that proved to be false or that were not backed up by Scripture? _____
_____
_____

Here's another example of biblical limitation—
People ask, "What did I do to deserve this?" The real question is, "What have I done wrong to be punished?" People asked questions like these in Jesus' day. Many Jews believed that sin caused suffering. Did Jesus believe all bad situations were the result of sin? See *John 9:1-3* and *Luke 13:1-5*.

How did Jesus feel about sin and tragedy? _____
_____

In *John*, Jesus eliminated sin as the cause of the man's suffering, pointing out that God could use suffering to show His power to heal. In *Luke*, Jesus used the tragedy to warn people to repent and to get right with God.

> **To correctly interpret Scripture you must be content with what God wants you to know. The serious Bible student does not find it necessary to demand from the Bible answers that are not there.**

Day 4
Apply the Bible Wisely, Part 1

A sk what the verse means.
P ractice the Bible as a book of standards.
P lug in the promises carefully
L earn about the culture.
Y ou must understand the technique of overstatement.

Today you study Rule 2—Apply the Bible Wisely. Here's an example of applying Scripture unwisely and incorrectly.

A group of new Christians from an Ethiopian tribe were visiting in a missionary home. One of the missionary's children bounded into the living

A STUDENT'S GUIDE TO STUDYING THE BIBLE

How's your Scripture memory going? Write what you've memorized of *1 Peter 5:6-7* here.

_____
_____
_____
_____
_____
_____
_____
_____
_____
_____

room with the family dog running behind. The small dog came near the visitors in a friendly fashion. The guests retreated in apparent fear.

"He won't harm you," the missionary reassured them. The guests told the missionary that they were not afraid of the dog. They just felt that Christians should not have dogs around them. Their biblical support for this belief was Paul's instruction to *"beware of dogs"* (*Phil. 3:2*, KJV). The missionary explained that Paul meant human beings who acted like dirty, vicious street dogs.[1] Paul had nothing against dogs. These zealous Christians had applied a verse in the wrong way because they had given it the wrong meaning.

The first guideline for applying the Bible to life is to **ask what the verse means.** As you know, some Scripture is more difficult to understand than others. You can learn the meaning of a verse by using modern English translations of the Bible, a commentary, and other Bible study tools.

Read *Ephesians 4:26*. What do you think Paul meant Christians should do about their anger? _____
_____

Paul recognized that people get angry when mistreated or when they see another person mistreated. Paul understood this kind of anger. But Paul warned that anger of any kind should not lead to sin.

How can you apply *Ephesians 4:26* to your life? _____
_____
_____

Read *1 Thessalonians 5:17*. Did Paul expect Christians to pray all the time? (Use a commentary for help.) _____
_____
_____

Praying without ceasing means to be in an attitude of prayer all the time. It doesn't have to be vocal prayer. It's a constant awareness of God's will for our lives. Paul wanted to motivate us to keep in touch with God.

How can you apply *1 Thessalonians 5:17* to your life? _____
_____

The second guideline for applying the Bible wisely is to **practice the Bible as a book of standards.** The Bible contains many standards on how to live and serve God. It warns against acts and attitudes that hinder following God. These directions and guidelines are general and broad, rather than detailed and specific. General, broad guidelines expand the Bible's message beyond a single time and a specific culture.

In *Acts 2:42-45* Luke, the author of *Acts*, described Christians who sold their possessions and shared the money with Christian friends.

Study this passage in a Bible commentary. Then, circle the statement that best expresses the standards of Luke's focus.
1. Christians should sell everything they have and share the money with other Christians.
2. Christians should not own private property.
3. The early church had a generous and unselfish spirit that all Christians should develop.
4. Christians who live in the same community must pool their resources.

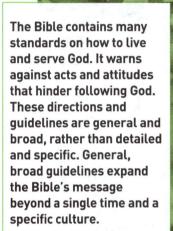

The Bible contains many standards on how to live and serve God. It warns against acts and attitudes that hinder following God. These directions and guidelines are general and broad, rather than detailed and specific. General, broad guidelines expand the Bible's message beyond a single time and a specific culture.

Did you circle number 3? These early Christians combined their resources to help those being persecuted for their belief. Many Christians suffered economically after accepting Christ. The Holy Spirit produced a spirit of generosity and unity in the church. Remember the guideline of using the Bible to interpret itself? No other Scripture commands Christians to sell their possessions and share the money with other Christians. Many passages, however, do call Christians to be unselfish and generous. (See *1 John 3:17*, for example).

What was the standard taught by the early Christians in *Acts 2:42-45*?
Standard: _____
_____

Now identify one way you can personally apply this standard.
Application: _____
_____

Read *1 Corinthians 8:13*. Does this mean that you should stop eating meat? Look in a commentary, then describe a general rule Paul stated for all Christians. _____
_____

The meat Paul wrote about had been part of a pagan sacrifice. Christians could purchase the unburned part of the meat at the market. However, some Christians felt that eating the meat endorsed paganism. Paul decided not to eat the meat to avoid hurting the faith of other Christians. There was nothing wrong with eating the meat, but other Christians saw the action as harmful. For this reason, Paul decided that he would not do anything that might harm the spiritual life of another Christian.

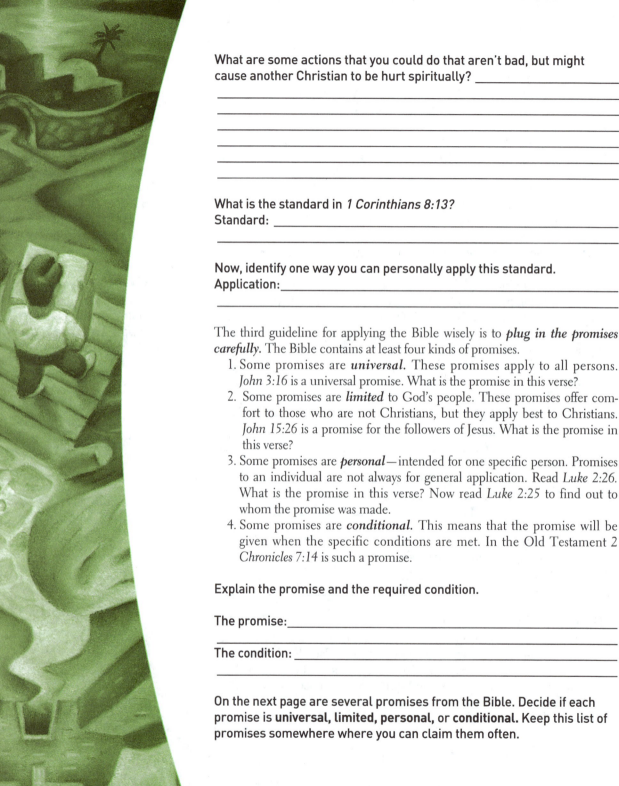

What are some actions that you could do that aren't bad, but might cause another Christian to be hurt spiritually? _____
_____
_____
_____
_____
_____
_____

What is the standard in *1 Corinthians 8:13?*
Standard: _____
_____

Now, identify one way you can personally apply this standard.
Application:_____
_____

The third guideline for applying the Bible wisely is to **plug in the promises carefully.** The Bible contains at least four kinds of promises.
1. Some promises are **universal.** These promises apply to all persons. *John 3:16* is a universal promise. What is the promise in this verse?
2. Some promises are **limited** to God's people. These promises offer comfort to those who are not Christians, but they apply best to Christians. *John 15:26* is a promise for the followers of Jesus. What is the promise in this verse?
3. Some promises are **personal**—intended for one specific person. Promises to an individual are not always for general application. Read *Luke 2:26.* What is the promise in this verse? Now read *Luke 2:25* to find out to whom the promise was made.
4. Some promises are **conditional.** This means that the promise will be given when the specific conditions are met. In the Old Testament *2 Chronicles 7:14* is such a promise.

Explain the promise and the required condition.

The promise:_____
_____

The condition: _____
_____

On the next page are several promises from the Bible. Decide if each promise is **universal, limited, personal,** or **conditional.** Keep this list of promises somewhere where you can claim them often.

PROMISE	TYPE	PROMISE	TYPE
Joshua 1:9	_____	Matthew 7:7	_____
Luke 13:12	_____	John 14:6	_____
1 Corinthians 10:13	_____	James 4:8	_____
2 Chronicles 7:14	_____	Luke 2:26	_____
John 3:16	_____	John 15:26	_____
Hebrews 13:5	_____	1 Peter 5:7	_____

This week's Scripture memory passage—*1 Peter 5:6-7*—is a promise to help you overcome worries that can defeat you. Write the verses from memory in the margin and identify the promise.

1 Peter 5:6-7 _____
_____
_____
_____
_____
_____
_____
_____
_____
_____
_____
_____
_____

Promise: _____
_____
_____
_____
_____
_____
_____

Day 5
Apply the Bible Wisely, Part 2

A sk what the verse means.
P ractice the Bible as a book of standards.
P lug in the promises carefully.
L earn about the culture.
Y ou must understand the technique of overstatement.

Read *John 13:14*. Jesus told the disciples to wash one another's feet. Now, look at *2 Corinthians 13:12*. Paul urged first-century Christians to greet each other with a holy kiss. As a Christian do you follow these commands? Probably not. Both might be misunderstood in today's society.

These commands applied to the first century. While we are not expected to imitate certain behavior, we are to live by the principle illustrated in the action.

What is the principle behind *2 Corinthians 13:12*? _____
_____
_____

Paul wanted his readers to show deep Christian love for one another. Today you show Christian love with a firm handshake, an appropriate hug, or an arm around someone's shoulder.

John 13:1-17 records that Jesus washed the feet of His disciples and urged them to wash one another's feet.

Why don't Christians wash each other's feet today? (Look in a Bible commentary to understand the custom of that day and why a person's feet needed to be washed.) What standard did Jesus teach with this event? How does this standard apply to your life?

Custom: _____

Standard: _____

Application:_____

In Jesus' time people walked around all day on dirty roads in open sandals. Their feet got filthy. Washing a guest's feet was usually done by a servant as a person entered a home. Since no servant was available to perform this courtesy at the last supper, Jesus became the servant and washed His disciples' feet.

Because we don't walk all day on dirt streets, we don't need to practice the act of foot washing today. We do need, however, to be kind and humble to others. Serving others is a modern example of washing feet.

So, here's the fourth guideline for applying the Bible wisely—*learn about the culture.* Although a certain command or action may seem strange today, it may have been appropriate at the time of the biblical writing. Take that action or command and look for the standard. Actions will change; standards remain eternal and universal.

Here's another example that shows the need to learn about the culture. Read the parable of the Good Samaritan in *Luke 10:30-37.* Jesus told this story to a prominent Jew who believed he was one of God's favored people. The parable shows the thoughtlessness of Jews. Only the Samaritan helped the wounded man. Look up *Samaritan* in a Bible dictionary to understand how the Jews felt about the Samaritans and vice versa.

Most Jews looked down on the Samaritans as a mixed race. The prejudiced Jews assumed that Samaritans felt the same way. Actually, the average Jew would have rejected any help from a Samaritan. A knowledge of first-century Jewish culture and attitudes makes this story more understandable to us.

This week's final guideline is that *you must understand the technique of overstatement.* Biblical writers and speakers used overstatement to make their points. Some commands in the Bible appear unreasonable until you see the overstatement.

TWO RULES TO GUIDE BIBLE STUDY

What overstatement did Jesus make in *Matthew 5:29?* _____
_____
_____

Jesus warned against committing sexual sin by looking at someone of the opposite sex in a lustful way. Did Jesus mean you should abuse your body by tearing out your right eye rather than be led to sin? Absolutely not! He overstated the situation for effect.

What did Jesus mean by His statement? _____
_____
_____

It isn't the eye that causes sin; evil thoughts and desires are the culprits. Jesus emphasized the need to use every effort to fight temptation. We must get rid of the things in our lives that cause us to sin.

What might be an overstatement today? Add your own examples.
"This day has been three years long."
"When he smiled, I thought I would die!"
_____
_____
_____

Here's one more example of overstatement—
  Peter asked Jesus how many times he had to forgive a person for sinning against him.

Read Jesus' reply in *Matthew 18:22,* then describe the overstatement and it's real meaning. _____
_____
_____

Peter felt that seven acts of forgiveness were sufficient. Jesus urged Peter to forgive again and again. The figure of seventy times seven symbolizes unlimited forgiveness, not an accounting of forgiveness.
  Congratulations for hanging in there! You've not only completed week 3, but you're halfway through this study. Let's see how you're doing. Complete the activity in the margin.

---
[1]Raymond Davis. *Fire on the Mountains* (SIM International, Toronto, 1980), 112. Used by permission.

Write the Scripture memory passages here.

Week 1: _____
_____
_____
_____
_____
_____
_____
_____
_____

Week 2: _____
_____
_____
_____
_____
_____
_____
_____
_____

Week 3: _____
_____
_____
_____
_____
_____
_____
_____
_____

Look at your hand. Identify what the thumb and first finger stand for?

Thumb: _____
_____
_____

First Finger: _____
_____
_____

This Week's Scripture Memory Passage
Do not be anxious about anything, but in everything, by prayer and petition, with thanksgiving, present your requests to God. And the peace of God, which transcends all understanding, will guard your hearts and your minds in Christ Jesus (Phil. 4:6-7).

This Week's Lessons
Day 1: Reading the Bible Continuously
Day 2: Big-Picture Bible Study
Day 3: Close-Up Bible Study, Part 1
Day 4: Close-Up Bible Study, Part 2
Day 5: Background Bible Study

Week 4
Three Ways to Do Bible Study

This week you will:
- learn how to study short books of the Bible and long Scripture passages in a broad, general way;
- learn how to study the Bible in a detailed, specific way;
- learn how to use background information to study the Bible.

THIS WEEK'S BIBLE STUDY TIP
When someone says "Bible study," you might have a mental image flash through your mind. Do you see yourself sitting in the middle of various Bible translations with commentaries, concordances, and Bible dictionaries piled around you? Is your computer flickering with information about your latest Bible challenge? Are you sitting, pencil in hand, ready to record the Bible's newest revelation? Isn't that what it's all about? Yes and no. Yes, because you are learning how to use the many resources and tools to help you unlock the easily understood and the not-so-easily understood passages of the Bible. But Bible study is more than resources and reference books, methods, and techniques. Effective Bible study begins and ends with prayer. Some people wait to pray until all else fails. How much more effective would Bible study be if you begin with prayer?

Include prayer in your Bible study. As you begin each session, pray that God will open your mind and heart to understand His Word. Pray that God will take away other thoughts that crowd into your mind so you can focus on Bible study. Close with a prayer of thanksgiving. Ask God to show you how to apply the verses you have studied to your life.

THREE WAYS TO DO BIBLE STUDY

Day 1
Reading the Bible Continuously

Read and mark *Philippians 4:6-7* **in your Bible. Use your Scripture memory card for week 4 to begin memorizing these verses.**

Check what you can learn about a city under each of these circumstances. If you **fly over** a city in an airplane, you can learn . . .
- 1. the overall size of the city;
- 2. what the structure of the city government is;
- 3. where teenagers hang out on weekends;
- 4. the amount of traffic in the city;
- 5. where the city is located in the country;
- 6. the type of land the city is built on;
- 7. the history of the city;
- 8. what sports teams represent the city;
- 9. how the people in the city compare to those in your hometown;
- 10. whether you would like to live in this city or not.

If you **walk around** a city and talk to the people, you can learn . . .
- 1. the overall size of the city;
- 2. what the structure of the city government is;
- 3. where teenagers hang out on weekends;
- 4. the amount of traffic in the city;
- 5. where the city is located in the country;
- 6. the type of land the city is built on;
- 7. the history of the city;
- 8. what sports teams represent the city;
- 9. how the people in the city compare to those in your hometown;
- 10. whether you would like to live in this city or not.

If you **research** the city, you can learn . . .
- 1. the overall size of the city;
- 2. what the structure of the city government is;
- 3. where teenagers hang out on weekends;
- 4. the amount of traffic in the city;

A STUDENT'S GUIDE TO STUDYING THE BIBLE

❑ 5. where the city is located in the country;
❑ 6. the type of land the city is built on;
❑ 7. the history of the city;
❑ 8. what sports teams represent the city;
❑ 9. how the people in the city compare to those in your hometown;
❑ 10. whether you would like to live in this city or not.

If you fly over a city, you will get a broad picture of the place. For example, you can see the overall size of a city, how the traffic flows, and the type of land on which the city is built.

If you walk through a city, you can look more closely at city life. You might find out where teenagers hang out by talking to several teenagers. You could tell what sports teams represent the city by checking out the stores or visiting local sports events. You can find out about the people and compare them to people in your hometown. You may even be able to make a personal judgment about whether you would like to live in this city.

If you research the city, you are looking for background information. Research gives you the history of the city, a look at the government structure, and information about the city's location.

Bible study happens in the same three ways—either a broad, general picture; a close up, detailed look; or through background information.

On the middle finger of the hand in the front of your book write "Three Ways to Do Bible Study."

BIG-PICTURE BIBLE STUDY
You can understand the Bible by getting an overview of a Bible book or a large portion of Scripture like the Sermon on the Mount. You get that overview by reading a short Bible book or a long, biblical passage at one time. Some people call this way of doing Bible study Synthetic Bible Study. (Synthesis is putting it all together.) You can call it Big-Picture Bible Study. Tomorrow you will look at this method more thoroughly.

CLOSE-UP BIBLE STUDY
Sometimes you will take a detailed look at the Bible. Maybe you want to study one person's story or a specific passage. You don't have to read the whole book to look closely at several verses of a book. Some people call this Bible study Analytical Bible Study. You can call it Close-Up Bible Study. On days 3 and 4 you will look at this method.

BACKGROUND BIBLE STUDY
You can better understand the Bible, the people in a specific story, or the circumstances concerning a Bible passage if you know basic background information. Who wrote the book (or passage)? Why was the book written?

THREE WAYS TO DO BIBLE STUDY

When was it written? What conditions surrounded the writing of the book? Why do similar stories have different details? How did the people's spiritual condition influence a passage? Some people call this Background Bible Study; you can, too! On day 5 you will look at what is involved in this method of Bible study.

Did you get the three ways? Without looking back, write them here:
1. B____-P_____ Bible Study
2. C____-U___ Bible Study
3. B_____ Bible Study

Let's try out what you've learned today. Look up each of the following Scriptures in your Bible. Beside each Scripture reference, decide if you could conduct a Big-Picture Bible study (write "1"), a Close-Up Bible study (write "2"), or a Background Bible study (write "3").

___ Philemon 1-25
___ Philippians 4:4-7
___ Ephesians 1:1
___ Psalm 98
___ Acts 17:1-9
___ Genesis 11:31—12:5
___ Ruth 1:1—4:22
___ 1 Samuel 17:4-10,45-50

This is how I would study these passages. I would use **Big-Picture Bible study** to understand *Philemon* and *Ruth*. I would use **Close-Up Bible study** for the passages from *Philippians*, *Psalms*, and maybe *1 Samuel*. I would use **Background Bible study** for the verses from *Ephesians*, *Acts*, and *Genesis*.

Look at this week's Scripture memory passage. Write these verses several times in the margin to begin memorizing them.

Day 2
Big-Picture Bible Study

Yesterday you saw that one way to study the Bible is to get the big picture. (This is also called Synthetic Bible Study, if you want to impress your friends.) **Big-Picture Bible Study** consists of reading a book in the Bible continuously, repeatedly, independently.

In other words, you read the Bible book or the large passage without stopping. Of course, you don't want to try this with *Exodus* or *Isaiah*. But, several books of the Bible can be read in one sitting. Look at *Jonah* or *Esther* in the Old Testament, and *Philippians* and *Titus* in the New Testament.

Flip through your Bible and find three more short books in the Bible that could be read in a brief amount of time. List them here.
1. _____
2. _____
3. _____

To read a Bible book or a large section of a book in the Bible, try these tips:
1. The first time, read the book like you would any other story or letter. Ignore chapter and verse divisions. This is called *continuous reading*.
2. You may need to read the book more than once. The second time slow down. Notice headings the Bible publisher inserted to help you understand sections of the story, history, or letter. This is called *repeated reading*.
3. Don't use a commentary or Bible study help at first. Let the Holy Spirit teach you. This is called *independently reading* the Bible.

Let's get started by actually trying out the Big-Picture approach. Read the book of *Philemon* in the New Testament at one time, straight through. Come back here when you're finished.

OK, let's focus on that first reading. Use these questions to evaluate what you've read. Make notes beside the questions or on a separate note pad. You will add to these notes during the week.
- What type of literature is in *Philemon*—poetry, prophecy, narrative, an epistle, or a combination of these? (Review week 3, day 1.)
- Why was the book written? Was it written to oppose sin, to deny a false teaching, or to confront indifference? If the writer didn't state a purpose, can you figure it out?
- How did the writer carry out his purpose? What ideas did the writer present to support his purpose?
- **To whom was the author writing—an individual or a group, persecuted Christians, wavering believers, or those who were confused?**
- What emotions are expressed in the passage? Joy? Concern? Excitement? Frustration?
- What words or phrases appear frequently?

The following example from the New Testament illustrates the assistance that the previous questions offer in evaluating what has been read. Let's look at *Philemon*. The book of *Philemon* was written to an individual Christian who owned a slave named Onesimus. The slave had run away from his master.

THREE WAYS TO DO BIBLE STUDY

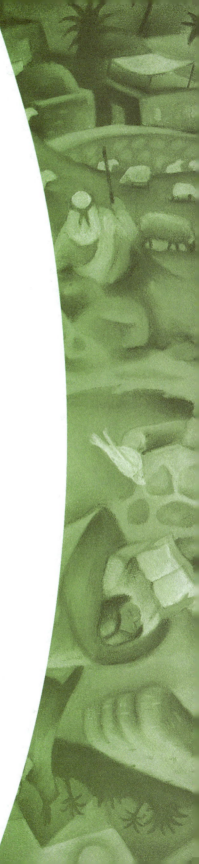

While he was AWOL, Onesimus met Paul and became a Christian. Paul sent Onesimus back to Philemon with an appeal that Onesimus be accepted as a brother in Christ and forgiven for his actions.

Read *Philemon* again. (Aren't you glad I chose a really short book?) If you have several modern translations of the Bible, read and compare the story in each of these. Notice how the verses are separated into paragraphs and headings.

Now, find a note pad or a sheet of paper. On it design a reading chart, or make an outline that identifies the verses and summarizes the information in the verses.

Making a chart gives you three major advantages:
1. It forces you to summarize the ideas of the book or passage you are studying.
2. It helps you see relationships between paragraphs.
3. It helps you remember the content of the book or passage.

Your reading chart might look like this. Record the chapter and verse titles on the chart as they are written in the Bible. This step helps you understand the teachings in the book of the Bible. Summarize each paragraph in an attempt to figure out the thoughts of the writer. I've filled in some of the information from the *New International Version* of the Bible to get you started. Make a summary statement or title for each division. (Note that since the book of *Philemon* is only one chapter the first two columns are blank.)

CHAPTER	CHAPTER TITLE	VERSES TITLE	VERSE	SUMMARY STATEMENT
			1-3	Greeting
			4-7	Thanksgiving and Prayer
			8-11	Paul's Plea for Onesimus
			12-16	
			17-22	
			23-25	

57

If you'd like to, compare your outline with another outline like the one in a Bible commentary. Your outlines won't match exactly but what you find in the commentary should resemble your efforts.

How many times should you read a book of the Bible? That depends on the length of the book, your understanding of the material, and the amount of time you have. Each time you read the book or passage, write down your questions. Then, as you continue to read and reread the book or passage look for answers to your questions. Each reading results in new, deeper insight into the truths of the book.

To see how a Big-Picture Bible study can help you with a large passage in the Bible, turn to *Matthew 5—7*. These three chapters are called the Sermon on the Mount. Get the big picture of these chapters by reading through them all at one time. On a clean sheet of paper, make an outline chart of this Sermon. The section headings reveal the topics that Jesus talked about. I've written in a few to get you started.

CHAPTER	CHAPTER TITLE	VERSES TITLE	VERSE	SUMMARY STATEMENT
5	None		1-12	The Beatitudes
5			13-16	Salt and Light

Day 3
Close-Up Bible Study, Part 1

When you paraphrase Scripture, you express the thoughts of the writer in your own words.

STOP. Take a sheet of paper and outline your hand on it. On the thumb, first, and middle fingers write three phrases that you've learned related to Bible study. OK, now you may continue. Yesterday you saw that the first way to do Bible study is with B_____-P_____ Bible study. This way lets you study a short book or a long, continuous passage of Scripture in one sitting.

Usually, however, you won't study an entire book of the Bible at one time. Most of the time you will study a short passage, or even one verse. To do this, use **Analytical Bible study**. When you analyze something, you look at it closely to understand the whole. I call this **Close-Up Bible study**. This type of Bible study has five elements. Today we'll look at three; tomorrow you'll check out the last two. The five elements are:
1. Make a Paraphrase.
2. Use Observations, Questions, and Answers.
3. Summarize the Content.
4. Make a Comparison.
5. Make it Personal.

PARAPHRASE
When you paraphrase Scripture, you express the thoughts of the writer in your own words. You have been memorizing *Philippians 4:6-7* as this week's Scripture memory passage.

Study the additional verses of *Philippians 4:4-7* in your Bible. These verses form a paragraph in most Bible translations. To paraphrase this paragraph, read the verses several times in different Bible translations. Notice the main nouns and verbs in the sentences. Underline key thoughts of the writer. On a separate sheet of paper write *Philippians 4:4-7* in your own words. Express the thoughts, attitudes, and purposes

A STUDENT'S GUIDE TO STUDYING THE BIBLE

of the biblical writer in words and phrases that you understand. Consider these questions to help you write your paraphrase.
- How is prayer emphasized?
- How does the command in *verse 6* relate to the promise in *verse 7*?
- What does "peace of God" mean in today's terminology?
- How can you express "hearts" and "minds" in *verse 7*?

Compare your paraphrase to a modern Bible translation.

OBSERVATIONS, QUESTIONS, AND ANSWERS

Another way to do Close-Up Bible study is to make observations about the Scripture. One method of observation identifies grammar and sentence elements like these:

- *Key Words* What do the verbs, nouns, adjectives, or adverbs mean?
- *Key Statements* Does a statement give advice, offer a warning, declare something, or make a promise?
- *Contrasts or Comparisons* What does the writer compare or contrast?
- *Repetition* What words or phrases are repeated?
- *Questions* Does a question in a passage introduce a new idea?
- *Connectives* Words like *but*, *if*, and *therefore* are there for a reason; what is it?
- *Grammar* Look at verb tenses and use of pronouns, adjectives, and adverbs.
- *Atmosphere* What is the general tone of the passage?
- *Literary Form* Is it poetry, prophecy, narrative, an epistle, or a parable?
- *General Organization* How are the ideas in the passage related to one another?

Read *Philippians 4:4-7* again and write down two or three observations in the margin using a few of these categories.

Another method of observation is to ask questions about the passage. You might ask *who* questions (Who wrote this material? For whom was the passage intended?), *what* questions (What is happening? What event created this situation?), *why* questions (Why did the writer say these things? Why is this thought emphasized?), and *so what* questions (So what does this passage mean to me today? So what do I do with this information?). Questions encourage you to look for answers and extend your study.

As you read *Philippians 4:4-7* look for questions that need answers. List at least one *who*, *what*, *why*, and *so what* question.

Who . . . _____

_____

What . . . _____

_____

Observations: _____
_____
_____
_____
_____
_____
_____
_____
_____
_____
_____
_____
_____
_____
_____
_____
_____
_____
_____
_____
_____
_____

THREE WAYS TO DO BIBLE STUDY

Why . . . _____
_____
So what . . . _____
_____

In order to find answers to your questions look in the Bible study tools you have been using.
- A regular dictionary helps you define unfamiliar words.
- Different Bible translations offer meaning to a phrase or puzzling statement.
- Look up passages that are cross-referenced in your study Bible.
- Check out a Bible dictionary, a concordance, or a commentary.
- Think, examine, meditate, and pray.

SUMMARIZE
A third way to do Close-Up Bible study is to write a summary. Your summary can be based on your paraphrase, observations, questions, and answers. The summary helps you express what you learn about a passage. It also prepares you to make the passage personal. There are two ways to summarize a passage—state conclusions or develop an outline.

Make your conclusions about what you have observed and questioned. You are trying to say what the biblical writer meant as he recorded words.

Use your paraphrase, observations, questions, and answers, to write a summary conclusion (two or three sentences) about *Philippians 4:4-7* in the margin.

Here is a sample summary. Compare your summary with this one—
Paul wanted to do more than tell the Philippians not to worry. He gave them a practical activity to do instead of worrying. They were to tell God what they needed.

The other way to summarize a passage is to develop an outline. This is similar to charting a book of the Bible, like you saw yesterday in the Big-Picture Bible study, except this outline is shorter. To make an outline, use the statements, commands, or questions of a paragraph as the main points.

Take one statement from each verse in *Philippians 4:4-7* and write a sentence outline.
Verse 4: Rejoice _____
_____
Verse 5: Let_____
_____
Verse 6: Do not _____
_____

> **The summary helps you express what you learn about a passage. It also prepares you to make the passage personal.**

Summary Conclusion:____
_____
_____
_____
_____
_____
_____
_____
_____
_____
_____
_____
_____
_____
_____

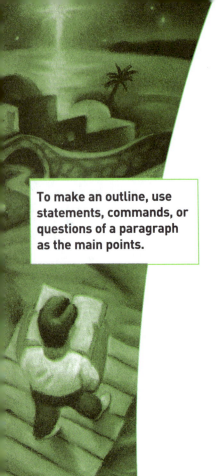

A STUDENT'S GUIDE TO STUDYING THE BIBLE

Verse 7: And the peace _____
_____

An outline helps you remember the words and meaning of the passage. You also could choose a single word for each part of your outline.

What four words would you choose from *Philippians 4:4-7*?
_____   _____
_____   _____

> To make an outline, use statements, commands, or questions of a paragraph as the main points.

After outlining a paragraph, give the paragraph a short title. Select words that reflect the message or teaching of the Bible passage. If possible, use words that come directly from the Bible. An outline and your conclusions summarize what you have learned about *Philippians 4:4-7*.

To conclude your Bible study time, thank God for three things that make you joyful. _____   _____   _____

Day 4
Close-Up Bible Study, Part 2

Do you remember the two ways to do Bible study you've studied so far? On day 2 you learned about B_____-P_____ Bible study. On day 3 you learned about C_____-U____ Bible study that involves five methods. The first three methods are P_____ ; O_____ , Q_____ , and A_____; S_____. Today you'll look at the final two methods of Comparing and Personalizing.

COMPARE
After you figure out the meaning of a Bible passage, compare the passage with other verses that teach or relate to the same message. This is called **comparative Bible study** because you make three comparisons:
• Topics or Subjects   • Persons or Events   • Words

THREE WAYS TO DO BIBLE STUDY

Continue to look at *Philippians 4:4-7* since you've already invested time in understanding this Scripture. (This also helps you memorize this week's Scripture memory passage.) To *compare by topics or subjects* ask two questions:
1. What subject or topic is being discussed in this passage?
2. What does this passage say about that topic?

Next, compare this information with what other passages say about the same subject. To find out what those other Scriptures contain about the subject, use several resources.
- *Your Bible* may list related verses in the margin or at the bottom of the page. Look for small numbers or letters beside key words in the Bible passage. These refer you to footnotes or marginal notes that give the related verses.
- Look in a *Bible concordance* under one or two of the key words from your Scripture passage.

Occasionally, you can locate related passages by looking up the topic in a *Bible dictionary*.

Yesterday, you gave *Philippians 4:4-7* a title. Use that title to compare. For example, if your title is "Stay Happy," look up words related to *happy (joy, rejoice, content)* in a Bible concordance to find related verses on the same theme. Or, if your title was "Don't Worry" look up *worry* in a Bible concordance. In the margin are several references on anxiety. After reading each verse, write a brief sentence describing how it relates to *Philippians*.

After you figure out the meaning of a Bible passage, compare the passage with other verses that teach or relate to the same message. This is *comparative Bible study*.

Psalm 55:22 _____
_____
_____
_____
_____

Matthew 6:25 _____
_____
_____
_____
_____

Luke 12:25 _____
_____
_____
_____
_____

If you study Scripture on the life of Christ, compare what the other Gospels say about the same incident. One Gospel may give more details than another. Comparing all the Gospels gives you a better idea of what Jesus said and did.

To *compare by using words,* you need a good concordance. Some concordances list every verse that contains your word; others list only a few familiar verses. Some words like *joy* and *prayer* have many references. Other words like *cake* may only have one or two verses. HINT—In addition to looking up the word or topic that you are studying, also look up synonyms (words or topics that mean the same) and antonyms (words or topics that are the opposite).

Look up the word *prayer* from *Philippians 4:6* in a concordance. Read three or four of the verses listed in the concordance. Notice how each verse compares to the idea of prayer in Philippians.

Compare using people and events. Often your study reveals people or events that illustrate the truth you are studying. A comparison helps you see how a biblical truth works in human experience. Use a Bible dictionary to pull together what is known about a person or a situation, in addition to the information in the Bible.

A STUDENT'S GUIDE TO STUDYING THE BIBLE

Lydia was Paul's first convert in the city of Philippi *(Acts 16:14)*. Find out about Lydia and her friendship with Paul by looking up her name in a Bible dictionary. List three things you learned about Paul and Lydia in the margin.

PERSONALIZE

Personalizing the Bible verses is the final way to study the Bible close up. Everything that you have studied this week brings you to this point of personal application. You've learned how to find the meaning of a passage. You've learned to evaluate what the verses are saying. You compared the passage to other passages that deal with the same subject. Now, apply the Scripture passage to your life.

When you apply the Bible to your life, be:
- *personal* (write sentences using *I*, *me*, or *my*);
- *practical* (select something you can do);
- *specific* (identify how the verses apply to you).

Here are several questions to help you personalize Bible study.
- What do I need to believe about God, Jesus Christ, the Holy Spirit, grace, mercy, forgiveness, hope, or eternal life?
- What do I need to do? Do I need to change an action or confess a sin? Do I need to get rid of attitudes such as fear, worry, hate, resentment, or jealousy? Do I need to develop an attitude of patience or humility?
- What have I learned about relationships? What does this passage teach me about my relationship with God through Jesus Christ? What new insights have I gained about my relationship with others in my family, community, congregation, or world?
- Is there a promise that I can claim? What are the conditions for claiming this promise? Are there words of encouragement or hope?

Using these questions as a guide, write in the space below several ways to personalize *Philippians 4:4-7*. Be practical and specific. After writing several statements, write your Scripture memory passage for this week on a separate sheet of paper.

1. _____
_____

2. _____
_____

3. _____
_____

THREE WAYS TO DO BIBLE STUDY

Day 5
Background Bible Study

Today you look at the final way to do Bible study—Background Bible Study. By studying the background of a Bible passage, you learn about the *history* related to an event, the *geography* of the land, the *culture* of the time, and the *sociology* of the people in the Scripture.

Here is one example of gathering background information. Read *Ephesians 1:1* and answer the questions in the margin.

Just one verse can reveal several background details. Paul wrote this letter to the saints (also known as Christians) in the city of Ephesus. Ephesus was located inside the border of today's country of Turkey. *Acts 19* contains cultural information about Ephesus.

HISTORY
History helps us understand the books of the Bible better. You can look at the history of one event or the history of a Bible book. You can research the history of one person, one city, or one nation. Other sections of the Bible provide historical information. For example, *Acts* tells us about Paul's life and ministry.

Check the background information about Paul's work in Thessalonica. Read *1 Thessalonians 1:6-10*, then in the margin summarize how Paul described the people in the church at Thessalonica.

Use a Bible dictionary or commentary to learn background information about Thessalonica. Look under the heading "Thessalonians, First Epistle to" or "Thessalonica" and answer the questions in the margin.

Study *Acts 17:1-11* to determine the historical relationship between Paul and the people of Thessalonica. The events of *Acts 17* took place on Paul's second missionary journey from A.D. 50-53.

Who wrote the book? _____

To whom was it written? (Look up *saints* in a Bible dictionary.) _____

Where did these Christians live? _____

In what country would that city be located today? (Compare a Bible map of Paul's missionary journeys with a map of Europe.) _____

Summary: _____
_____
_____
_____
_____
_____
_____

Thessalonica was the capital of what Roman province? _____

Why was Thessalonica an important city in Paul's day? _____

What kind of relationship did Thessalonica have with the Roman emperor? _____

A STUDENT'S GUIDE TO STUDYING THE BIBLE

How did Paul begin his ministry in Thessalonica? *(vv. 2-3)* _____

Who helped Paul? Who responded to Paul's message? *(vv. 4)* _____

How did the Jews respond to Paul? *(vv. 5-7)* _____

Where did Paul go when he left Thessalonica? *(v. 10)* _____

GEOGRAPHY

Geography teaches the location of cities, the significance of rivers, lakes, and seas, and other prominent features of the land such as mountains. It shows how geography influences the people and their stories. For example, geography played an important role in *John 4:1-5*.

Read *John 4:1-5* then answer the questions in the margin.

Where was Jesus leaving? _____

Where was Jesus going? _____

What land did Jesus pass through on His way? _____

Look at a map of Palestine (today, called Israel) in Jesus' time. Judea is located in southern Palestine; Galilee, in northern Palestine. Samaria lay between the two provinces. However, Jews avoided going through Samaria even though it was the shortest and quickest route. Instead, Jews crossed over the Jordan River into Perea to avoid Samaria. *John 4:4* indicates that Jesus "had to go through Samaria." Jesus' action startled His disciples, but look at what happened. As you skim *John 4* you'll recognize the familiar story of the woman at the well. You'll find the reason why Jesus had to go through Samaria in *John 4:39-41*.

How does knowing the geographical information improve the story? ___

CULTURE

Learning about a people's culture involves studying that civilization's religion, science, music, art, literature, drama, and philosophy. Bible commentaries are the best source for examining Bible culture. Information about the culture explains many passages in the Bible. Here's an example of how knowledge of a culture can make Bible study more vivid and accurate.

Read *John 2:13-18*. Look in a Bible commentary to find why the Jews were so threatened by Jesus and His actions.

Culturally, the practice of exchanging one kind of money for another in the temple area was accepted among the Jews. Jesus felt that the temple was not the proper place for this activity. The Jews challenged Jesus' authority to drive the moneychangers from the temple. Jesus' response to the Jews' challenge in *John 2:19* is puzzling unless you understand the culture. Look up this verse in a Bible commentary.

THREE WAYS TO DO BIBLE STUDY

Read *John 2:20-22*. Now, find "Temple of Herod" or "Herod's Temple" in a Bible dictionary.

What did the Jews think Jesus was talking about? _____
_____

What was Jesus talking about? _____
_____

For centuries the Jews had a small, fortress-like structure to use for worship. It began under the Old Testament leader Zerubbabel (*Ezra 3:8*), but it was not as beautiful as the temple of Solomon. Herod the Great, who reigned over Palestine from 37-4 B.C., expanded Zerubbabel's temple into a magnificent temple made of huge blocks of white stone to please the Jews. He started his project around 19 B.C. *John 2:20* reveals that the actual work lasted for 46 years. Any threat against their place of worship was considered blasphemy. Later, the Jewish leaders tormented Jesus with His supposed threat against the temple as He hung on the cross (*Matt. 27:40*).

Of course, Jesus was not referring to the Jews' temple, but to His body.

SOCIOLOGY
Sociology studies human behavior and relationships of groups. This provides information about family, towns and cities, government, religion, race, travel, business, and social classes.

Earlier this week you studied Philemon. This letter reveals information about the practice of slavery in the first century and how that practice affected the church.

Look up *slave* or *slavery* in a Bible dictionary. Write in the margin an explanation of slavery in Paul's time.

Under Roman law a slave owner could brutally punish a runaway. In addition, whoever gave refuge to a runaway was expected to pay the owner for each day of lost work time. When Paul told Philemon in *verse 18* to charge to him anything that Onesimus owed, he may have been promising to repay Philemon for the time when Onesimus was a runaway. Read *Philemon 15-16* to discover what Paul hoped Philemon would do with Onesimus.

Paul did not campaign against slavery, but he did attempt to establish an attitude in the church that would eventually do away with slavery. Asking Philemon to accept Onesimus as a Christian brother was a bold act in the first century.

Check-up time! Complete the worksheet in the margin.

Slavery in Paul's Time: ___
_____
_____
_____
_____
_____

This week you looked at Three W____ to D _____ B_____ S _____

The first way is B _____ -P_____ Bible Study (Synthetic Bible Study).

The second way is C_____-U_____ Bible Study (Analytical Bible Study). There are five methods to this type of Bible study. They are:
1. _____
2. _____
3. _____
4. _____
5. _____

The third way is B _____ Bible Study that looks at h_____ , g_____ , c_____ , and s_____.

Write this week's Scripture memory passage here. _____
_____
_____
_____
_____
_____
_____

This Week's Scripture Memory Passage

Consider it pure joy, my brothers, whenever you face trials of many kinds, because you know that the testing of your faith develops perseverance. Perseverance must finish its work so that you may be mature and complete, not lacking anything (Jas. 1:2-4).

This Week's Lessons

Day 1: Introducing Biblical Application for Four Areas of Life
Day 2: Applying Biographical Bible Study
Day 3: Applying Character Trait Bible Study
Day 4: Applying Devotional Bible Study
Day 5: Practicing Application of the Bible to Life

Week 5
Four Areas to Apply Bible Study

This week you will:
- learn how to apply your Bible study to your relationship with God, your understanding of yourself, your relationships with others, and your relationship to the church;
- use the method of Biographical Bible Study to apply the Bible to life;
- use the method of Character Trait Bible Study to apply the Bible to life;
- use the method of Devotional Bible Study to apply the Bible to life.

THIS WEEK'S BIBLE STUDY TIP

Are you Internet active? If you don't own a personal computer, go to a public library (most have online computers), or stay after school and ask to use your school's computer lab. The Internet offers a wealth of Bible information. Like other parts of the Internet, some information is very helpful, while other sites are more confusing than helpful.

An excellent starting place for finding information to help you understand the Bible is the website *www.goshen.net*. This site has numerous links to other Christian sites. Another site is *www.bibleontheweb.com*. Through these sites you can look at several Bible translations to help you understand a verse. You also will find concordances, Bible dictionaries, and Bible commentaries. Type in a Bible reference to locate information about any verse. Ask a question and receive answers from people who study the Bible professionally. Don't ignore the Internet as a mighty tool in Bible study.

FOUR AREAS TO APPLY BIBLE STUDY

Day 1
Introducing Biblical Application for Four Areas of Life

> Read and mark *James 1: 2-4* in your Bible. Use your Scripture memory card to begin memorizing these verses.

Today you begin the fourth major focus on how to study the Bible. Looking at your own hand (not the one you drew in the front of the book), name the first three areas you have studied so far.

The thumb represents _____

The first finger represents _____

The middle finger represents _____

On the ring finger of the hand you drew in this book write "Biblical Application for Four Areas of Life." That's the focus for this week.

The purpose of all Bible study is to lead you to apply its teachings to your life. In week 3 you looked at five guidelines for applying the Bible wisely to life. These guidelines will help as you apply God's Word to four areas of your life.

> If you look at Bible study as a way to change your life suddenly the Bible becomes a powerful part of what you do, how you think, what you feel, and what you believe. Transforming Bible study is what application means.

Review these guidelines by filling in the blanks. If you need to look back, check out days 4 and 5 in week 3.

1. A _____ what the verse m _____.
2. P _____ the Bible as a book of s _____.
3. P _____ in the p_____ carefully.
4. L _____ about the c_____.
5. Y _____ must understand the technique of o _____.

Last week you looked at doing Bible study using the big picture method, the close-up method, and through a background study. These methods emphasize the importance of getting the facts and understanding the settings of the Bible. All this information is useful, but it won't change your life unless you apply what you learn. Without application Bible study will grow dead and lifeless.

A STUDENT'S GUIDE TO STUDYING THE BIBLE

Transform: _____
_____
_____
_____
_____
_____
_____
_____
_____
_____
_____

Look up "transform" in a regular dictionary. Write a couple of definitions in the margin.

How do you think the Bible can transform your life? _____
_____

You can apply the Bible to life in these four areas or relationships.
• God   • Self   • Others   • Church

YOUR RELATIONSHIP TO GOD
First, apply the Bible to your relationship with God. The Bible can help you form your beliefs about God, Jesus Christ, the Holy Spirit, sin, forgiveness, and eternal life. The Bible can direct you on what you can do for God, such as choosing a vocation or using your time in ministry or service. When you are tuned into God through His Word, all beliefs and actions will reflect your desire to glorify God and to follow His will for your life.

Read *Colossians 3:17* and write down two or three words that explain your relationship to God. _____
_____

YOUR UNDERSTANDING OF YOURSELF
Second, apply the Bible personally. The Bible convicts of personal sins that you must confess to God. It describes attitudes of hate, pride, worry, and fear to overcome. It challenges you to search for peace, joy, obedience, and love as you live for God. Of all the applications of Bible study, this personal one can be the hardest and the most rewarding.

Read *1 John 1:7-9* and write down a few words or phrases that express a personal application of the Bible. _____
_____

YOUR RELATIONSHIP WITH OTHERS
Apply the Bible to your relationships with others. The Bible presents ideas on how to act and think towards others. It teaches you to show forgiveness to members of your family, to express concern for friends, to witness to classmates, to respect teachers and coaches, and to make neighbors as important as yourself. It calls for you to express Christ's love to your enemies, to closest friends, even to casual acquaintances.

Read *John 13:34-35* and write down how you can show others that you are a servant of Christ. _____
_____

YOUR RELATIONSHIP WITH THE CHURCH

The fourth area where you can apply the Bible is in your relationship with the church, God's people on earth. God wants the church to reflect His purity, love, and compassion. Jesus believed that the church was the way for Christians to survive the chaos of this world. The church is a vital relationship in the life of every Christian.

Read *Ephesians 4:11-16* and write a few words or phrases that describe the importance of the church in a person's life. _____
_____

When you learn something about God, you often learn something about yourself, your relationships with others, and the church.

As you apply the Scriptures to these four areas, you will see that they frequently overlap. When you learn something about God, you often learn something about yourself, your relationships with others, and the church. As you focus on applying the Bible to these four areas this week, you will see how the Bible becomes alive and relevant.

Use this week's Scripture memory passage *James 1:2-4* to test how to apply the Bible to these four areas of life. After reading the verses ask,

HOW DOES THIS APPLY:

—to my relationship with God?	—to understanding myself?
_____	_____
_____	_____
_____	_____
—to my relationship with others?	—to my relationship with the church?
_____	_____
_____	_____
_____	_____

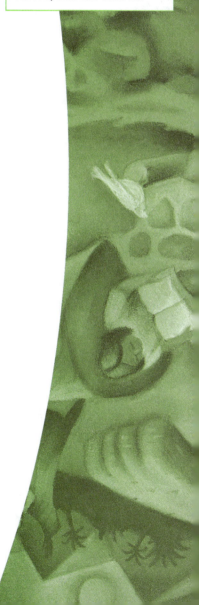

This week as you look at how to apply the Bible to these four areas, you also will learn three more methods of Bible study. First, you'll look at **Biographical Bible Study**. This Bible study looks at the lives of people in the Bible so you can learn from their experiences. Second, you'll look at **Character Trait Bible Study**. This Bible study attempts to identify the specific traits that the Bible encourages or condemns. You will study traits or qualities rather than a person's entire life. A third way to do Bible study is through **Devotional Bible Study**. This type of study emphasizes the use of the Bible to change lives.

Day 2
Applying Biographical Bible Study

List four areas of life where you can apply the Bible (from yesterday).
1. _____
2. _____
3. _____
4. _____

Today you will examine Biographical Bible Study as one method to use in applying the Bible to life. This method looks at the lives of people in the Bible in order to learn from their experiences. You can imitate their positive experiences and avoid their faults.

The Scriptures indicate that God gave us the stories of the Old Testament to serve as _____ for us. (Find the missing word in *1 Cor. 10:6.*)
These stories can _____ us. (Find the missing word in *Rom. 15:4.*)

There are four principles for doing Biographical Bible Study.
Principle 1—*Begin with a simple character.* Choose a person who can be defined quickly through a few biblical references. People like Barnabas, Priscilla, and Aquila appear only a few times in the Bible. Other people like Moses, David, and Paul appear many times and are more difficult to study. Work up to these more complex biographical studies as you become more skilled in Bible study.

Principle 2—*Watch for name changes.* Don't confuse identities. The Bible contains stories about many people named Mary, James, and John. Be sure you gather information about the same person. Also, some people are known by more than one name. Mark, the writer of the second Gospel, is also known as (AKA) John and John Mark. To gather facts about people with more than one name, look for all their names in a Bible dictionary, Bible encyclopedia, or a concordance.

Check out the different names for these people using a Bible dictionary or concordance.
Abraham AKA _____
Silas AKA _____
Peter AKA _____
Jacob AKA_____

Principle 3—*You can't locate all the information about a person just by looking up verses that contain a person's name.* For example, the Books of 1 and 2 Timothy provide information about Timothy, even though his name is not mentioned in every verse. Information about Joshua appears throughout the Book of Joshua, even in paragraphs where Joshua's name is not mentioned.

Principle 4—*Think about what it would have been like to live in a Bible person's circumstances.* After you learn about the customs and culture where the person lived, try to imagine how he or she felt and thought. Look at how the person responded to circumstances.

After you learn about the customs and culture of the place where the person lived, try to imagine how the Bible person felt and thought. Look at how the person responded to circumstances.

A BIOGRAPHICAL STUDY
Ready to try a Biographical Study of a Bible character? Let's look at John Mark, the writer of the Gospel of Mark. If you look up John Mark (also John and Mark separately) in a Bible concordance you would find several Scripture references including these—*Acts 12:12,25; 13:13; 15:37-39; Colossians 4:10; 2 Timothy 4:11; Philemon 24; 1 Peter 5:13.* Some Bible scholars believe John Mark is the anonymous youth mentioned in *Mark 14:51-52.*

Use a separate sheet of paper to make a worksheet for this study.
- List each verse or passage that refers to John Mark.
- Read each Scripture.
- Write any questions or observations related to these verses. Include questions you have about the person, the person's positive or negative traits, and any situations mentioned in the verses.
- Make an outline of John Mark's life. Sometimes you will find enough information to make a chronological outline. Other times your outline will list the places where the person lived or traveled. You may not have enough information to make a complete outline, but try to use what you have. A Bible dictionary can explain how some verses relate to the whole situation. Here's an example of an outline for John Mark. Write in the verses that relate to each event.

I. Home Background and Early Life
II. Opportunity for Service
III. Failure
IV. Comeback

A STUDENT'S GUIDE TO STUDYING THE BIBLE

After outlining the life of Mark, identify his positive and negatives traits. Look for things like his general reputation, aims and motives, family and country background, relationships with other people, general personality traits, and his spiritual life. Include this information in your outline.
- Summarize what you have learned about Mark.
- Finally, apply what you have learned about John Mark to the four areas of life that you looked at yesterday. Be specific in your application. I have written one application below to get you started. Think about your own life in relationship to John Mark's life.

What in the life of John Mark could apply to your relationship to God?
_____
_____

What in the life of John Mark could apply to your understanding of yourself? _____
_____

What in the life of John Mark could apply to your relationship to others? (Example: *I need to develop close personal relationships like the one between Barnabas and Mark.*) _____
_____

What in the life of John Mark can help you with your relationship to the church? _____
_____

Day 3
Applying Character Trait Bible Study

Your ultimate goal in Bible study is to become more and more like the Lord Jesus. One aim for every Christian is to develop godly character traits. Character Trait Bible Study identifies specific traits that the Bible encourages, as well as those it condemns. After identifying the traits, you

FOUR AREAS TO APPLY BIBLE STUDY

depend on the power of God to produce those positive traits in your life and to help you avoid the negative traits.

Unlike Biographical Bible Study you examine character traits or qualities, rather than the entire life of a person. Use these steps in a Character Trait Bible Study.

Step 1—Identify the trait you want to study. Select a trait that you desire in your own life. Or, choose an action or attitude that you want to learn about so you can eliminate it from your life. Let's study *James 1:2-4*, this week's Scripture memory passage.

Select a trait from these verses that you desire and write it here.
_____

Step 2—Find the meaning of the trait in a regular dictionary.

Write a definition of the word here. _____
_____

> **Unlike Biographical Bible Study you examine character traits or qualities, rather than the entire life of a person.**

Step 3—List synonyms of the word. Remember that synonyms are words that are similar to the main word you are studying. Listing synonyms broadens your understanding of the trait.

List several synonyms. _____
_____

Step 4—List antonyms of the trait. Antonyms are words that are opposite to the main character trait you are studying. A dictionary may identify several antonyms, including traits that have two or more opposites. For example, the opposite of *joy* could be *sorrow*. Or, it could be *worry, self-pity,* or *resentment*.

Write a few antonyms here. _____
_____

Step 5—Discover the Bible definition and teachings about the trait. Use a word concordance or a topical concordance to find passages in which the word appears. Some words can also be found in a Bible dictionary, along with the related verses.

Study and summarize each passage of related Scripture.

Step 6—Think about the character trait you are studying. Use questions like the following to guide your thinking. Write brief answers for the character trait you are studying today.

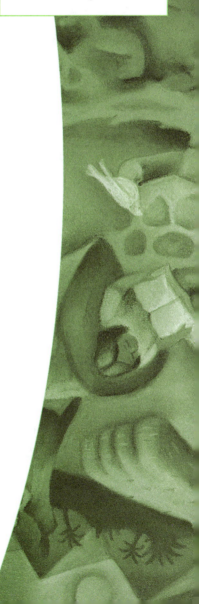

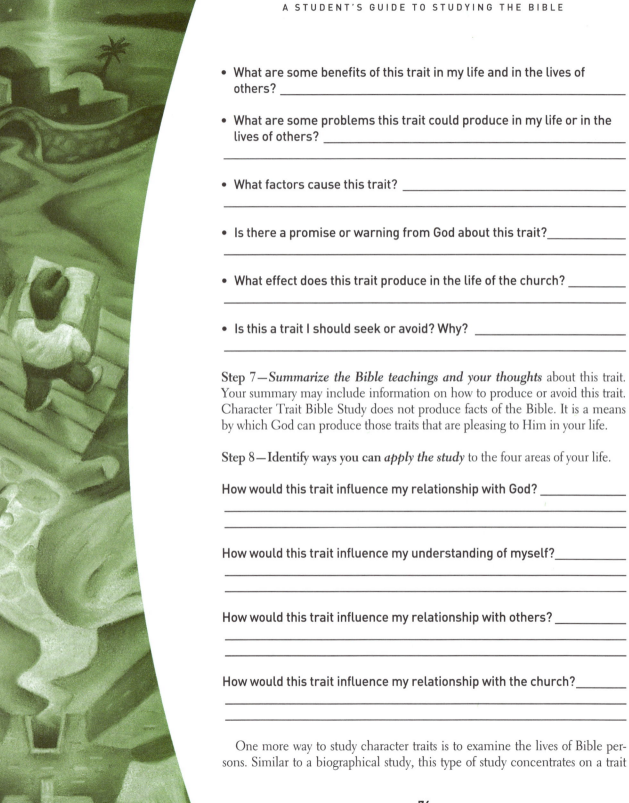

- What are some benefits of this trait in my life and in the lives of others? _____

- What are some problems this trait could produce in my life or in the lives of others? _____
  _____

- What factors cause this trait? _____
  _____

- Is there a promise or warning from God about this trait?_____
  _____

- What effect does this trait produce in the life of the church? _____
  _____

- Is this a trait I should seek or avoid? Why? _____
  _____

Step 7—*Summarize the Bible teachings and your thoughts* about this trait. Your summary may include information on how to produce or avoid this trait. Character Trait Bible Study does not produce facts of the Bible. It is a means by which God can produce those traits that are pleasing to Him in your life.

Step 8—Identify ways you can *apply the study* to the four areas of your life.

How would this trait influence my relationship with God? _____
_____
_____

How would this trait influence my understanding of myself?_____
_____
_____

How would this trait influence my relationship with others? _____
_____
_____

How would this trait influence my relationship with the church?_____
_____
_____

One more way to study character traits is to examine the lives of Bible persons. Similar to a biographical study, this type of study concentrates on a trait

FOUR AREAS TO APPLY BIBLE STUDY

or characteristic of the person, rather than on the life of the person. (For example, you might study the disciple Thomas' doubt.) Use the same steps as suggested, but study the person, as well as a particular trait.

How do you find Bible people with a particular trait you want to study? First, draw from your own knowledge of the Bible. You may be surprised at how easy it is to associate different Bible people with specific character traits. Look for characteristics as you research other Bible passages.

See how many Bible personalities you can match with their related character traits. Look at the Bible reference and in a Bible dictionary for persons you don't recognize. The answers are at the end of today's study.

CHARACTERISTIC MATCH-UP

___ 1. Dorcas *(Acts 9:36)*   a. Love
___ 2. Sapphira *(Acts 5:1-2)*   b. Forgiveness
___ 3. King Saul *(1 Sam. 18:28-29)*   c. Encouragement
___ 4. The apostle John *(2 John 5-6)*   d. Devotion
___ 5. Ruth *(Ruth 1:16-17)*   e. Courage
___ 6. Peter *(Acts 4:18-20,31)*   f. Wisdom
___ 7. Barnabas *(Acts 11:22-24)*   g. Bold
___ 8. Joshua *(Josh. 1:1-6)*   h. Kindness
___ 9. Solomon *(1 Kings 3:5-9)*   i. Jealousy
___ 10. Hosea *(Hos. 3:1-2)*   j. Deceit

A character trait I would like to study is... _____

A biblical person with a character trait I would like to study is... _____
_____

(Answers to Characteristic Match-Up: 1-h; 2-j; 3-i; 4-a; 5-d; 6-g; 7-c; 8-e; 9-f; 10-b.)

A STUDENT'S GUIDE TO STUDYING THE BIBLE

Day 4
Applying Devotional Bible Study

Write this week's Scripture memory passage here. ____
_____
_____
_____
_____
_____
_____
_____
_____
_____
_____
_____

Today you will learn how to do a Devotional Bible Study. You will apply what you learn to your relationship with God, to your life, to your relationship with others, and to your relationship with the church. This method emphasizes how the Bible can change lives. Remember in week 4 when you studied Close-Up Bible Study? That method emphasized identifying facts and truths in the Bible. In Devotional Bible Study, the primary emphasis is on application. You still want to look at the details of a passage, but your primary focuses is a desire to do God's will and to let the message of God change your life. Keep these guidelines in mind.

Guideline 1—Learn the correct meaning of a verse or chapter in the Bible. If you misunderstand what a passage is saying, your application will be wrong. Check your understanding by comparing your summary statements about the verses with a Bible commentary. For example, in week 3, day 4 you saw how to interpret Paul's words in *Ephesians 4:26*. (Look at what you wrote.) Righteous anger exists. Paul knew righteous anger can change quickly into uncontrolled, selfish anger. Paul warned against letting this anger get out of control.

Guideline 2—Determine if a passage is talking about a timeless truth or a temporary application. Timeless principles or truths apply to all people, anytime, under all circumstance. Temporary applications deal with a specific circumstance, person, or problem.

In week 3, day 5 you learned that some passages present a standard to follow, rather than an action to imitate. Remember the standard in *2 Corinthians 13:12*? (Look at what you wrote.) Some passages describe conditions that you won't face in today's world. In those cases, apply the principle, not the action.

Guideline 3—Relate the passage to other passages that teach the same truth. In week 3, day 2 you saw how Jesus' teaching about prayer in *Matthew 21:22* needs to be understood in relationship to *James 4:3* and *1 John 5:14-15*.

FOUR AREAS TO APPLY BIBLE STUDY

Guideline 4—Reflect on various areas where a passage can be applied. The standard or truth may apply to:
• your religious life,
• your personal attitudes and actions,
• your social life,
• your family life, or
• any other area of your life.

Biblical insights might change your attitudes and relationships to
• fellow students,
• teachers,
• coaches,
• neighbors,
• even enemies.

Devotional Bible Study can help you:
• set goals,
• affirm your present activities,
• show you how to follow Christ, or
• challenge you to a commitment to follow God's will.

DEVOTIONAL BIBLE STUDY
Let's apply what you've learned about Devotional Bible Study to *Ephesians 4:32*. Use this work space to record the results of your study.

Summarize the meaning or teaching in the passage. _____
_____
_____
_____

Determine the type of application—timeless or temporary? Write a brief explanation of why you think this is true. _____
_____
_____
_____

Find related Bible passages. _____
(To determine this, look up the word *forgiveness* in a Bible concordance. Write the Scripture reference and a related truth for each Scripture.)

Reflect on the main truth and write it here. _____
_____
_____

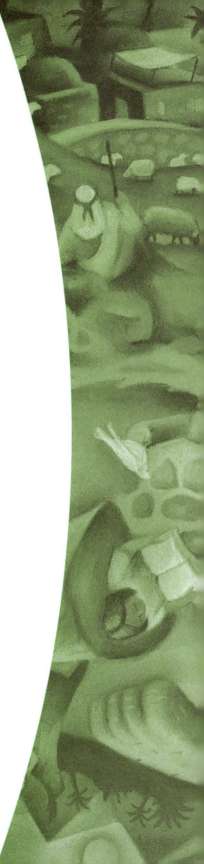

A STUDENT'S GUIDE TO STUDYING THE BIBLE

Apply this truth to these four areas of your life.
My relationship with God... _____
_____
_____

My understanding of myself... _____
_____
_____

My relationship with others... _____
_____
_____

My relationship to the church... _____
_____
_____

Day 5
Practicing Application of the Bible to Life

Time to review. Through the course of this study you have examined several Bible study ideas that can be remembered easily by simply using the first four fingers of your hand. Let's see how you're doing. These Bible study ideas are:

Thumb: One Bible Study P_____: A S_____ H_____

First Finger: Two R_____ to G_____ Bible Study
Rule 1: I_____ the Bible C_____.
Rule 2: A _____ the Bible W_____.

FOUR AREAS TO APPLY BIBLE STUDY

Middle Finger: Three W____ to D____ Bible Study
First Way: B___-P_____ Bible Study
Second Way: C____-U_____ Bible Study
Third Way: B_____ Bible Study

Ring Finger: Four A_____ to A____ Bible Study
Your Relationship to _____
Your Understanding of Y_____
Your Relationship with _____
Your Relationship with the _____

This week you've also looked at three more ways to approach Bible study. They are: B___-P_____ Bible study, C_____-U_____ Bible study, and B_____ Bible study.

One more thing to review. How are you doing on each week's Scripture memory passages? So far, you should have memorized five.

Here's a key word from each week's Scripture memory passage. Write the related biblical reference beside the key word. Then, on a separate sheet of paper, write out each Scripture memory passage.

Week 1 "light to the eyes" _____

Week 2 "spiritually discerned" _____

Week 3 "humble yourselves" _____

Week 4 "peace of God" _____

Week 5 "pure joy" _____

Today select one of the three Bible study methods you've studied this week to examine the Bible. Write your study on a separate sheet of paper. The following outlines of each study method should help you make your selection.

BIOGRAPHICAL BIBLE STUDY
- Select a biblical person you would like to study.
- Use a Bible concordance or topical Bible to find verses related to this person.
- Use these verses or passages to record information about the person you selected.
- Write down questions or observations related to each Scripture.

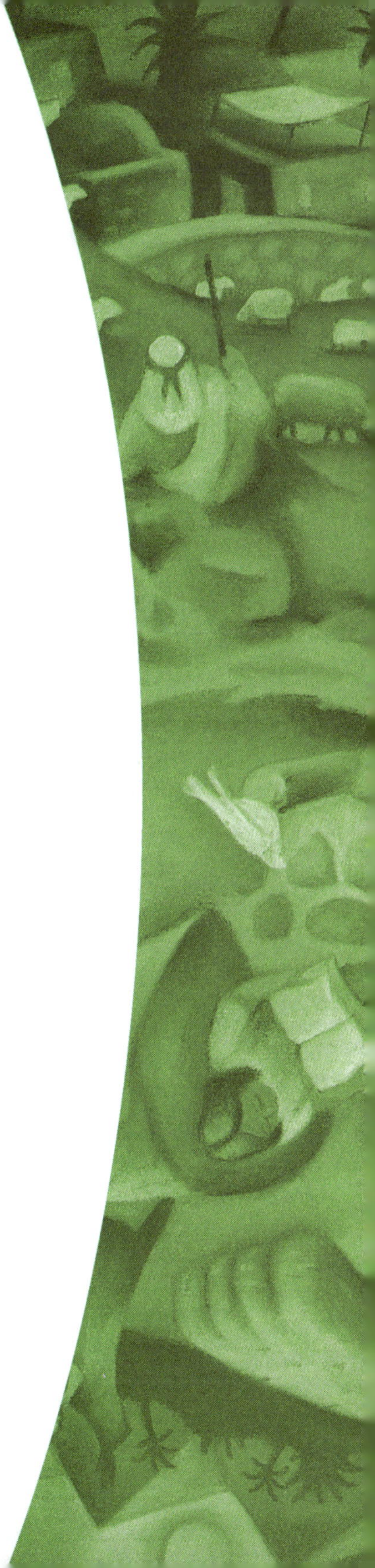

A STUDENT'S GUIDE TO STUDYING THE BIBLE

- Briefly outline this person's life using a Bible dictionary.
- Write a brief summary of this person's life.
- Apply what you have learned about this person to the four areas of life:
  a) Your relationship to God
  b) Your understanding of yourself
  c) Your relationship to others
  d) Your relationship to the church

CHARACTER TRAIT BIBLE STUDY
- Look at the trait of encouragement. First, define encouragement using a regular dictionary definition.
- List synonyms and antonyms of encouragement.
- Find out what the Bible says about encouragement by looking up several verses in a Bible concordance. Write a definition of encouragement according to the Bible. _____
_____

- To find an example of encouragement, look in a topical concordance. Did you see that Barnabas is an example of encouragement? In fact, Barnabas' name meant "an encourager."

Study these passages and summarize the ways Barnabas demonstrated the trait of encouragement.

Acts 9:26-27 _____
_____

Acts 11:22-26 _____
_____

Acts 15:36-39 _____
_____

- Use these questions to help you identify ways to apply the trait of encouragement to your life.

What is there in the life of Barnabas that I would like to have? _____
_____
How would this character trait affect my relationship with others? _____
_____
What results would this character trait produce in my relationship with God? _____
_____

FOUR AREAS TO APPLY BIBLE STUDY

How might this character trait affect my relationship to the church?
_____

DEVOTIONAL BIBLE STUDY
- Do a devotional Bible study on *Lamentations 3:22-23.* Summarize the meaning or teaching of the passage. _____
_____
_____

- Decide if the application is timeless or temporary and why. _____
_____
_____

- Relate the Scripture to other Bible passages. Look up these verses:

Psalm 84:11 _____
_____

Psalm 118:24 _____
_____

Romans 8:28-31 _____
_____

- Be sure you understand the meaning of *mercy.* Write down one worry or fear that bothers you. _____
_____
_____

How can God's mercy and faithfulness help you? _____
_____

How can this Scripture help you in your relationship with God? _____
_____

How can this Scripture help you in your relationship with others? _____
_____

How can this Scripture help you in your relationship with the church?
_____
_____

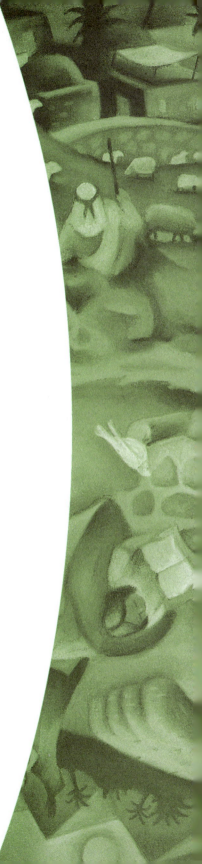

This Week's Scripture Memory Passage
Ask and it will be given to you; seek and you will find; knock and the door will be opened to you (Matt. 7:7).

This Week's Lessons

Day 1: Understanding the Words of the Bible
Day 2: Understanding the Images of the Bible
Day 3: Understanding the Grammar of the Bible
Day 4: Understanding the Topics of the Bible
Day 5: Understanding the Doctrines of the Bible

Week 6
Five Helps in Doing Bible Study

This week you will:
- examine how words have changed from biblical times to today;
- evaluate the images of the Bible as expressed in figures of speech;
- determine how grammar influences Bible passages;
- consider how to choose a topic for a Topical Bible Study;
- choose a theological teaching in order to do a Doctrinal Bible Study.

THIS WEEK'S BIBLE STUDY TIP
This week you graduate from this how-to-study-the-Bible workbook. For six weeks you've used this book as a place to record what you've learned. What are you going to do after this week? I hope you'll want to continue to learn. Keeping a Bible study notebook disciplines you to continue your study. Your notebook can be loose-leaf or spiral bound. Do you need a large notebook to record your thoughts and ideas or a small one to fit into your Bible?

In the notebook keep up with the Scripture passages you study, list the names of the people you look at, catalog specific applications you make to life, set goals for Bible study, and record prayer requests.

Set up your notebook anyway you want. For example, keep a day to day account. Or, title one page "Promises"; another page, "Challenges"; another, "People of the Old Testament." Record the verses that relate to each topic. Continue to choose verses to memorize each week. List the Bible studies you would like to do in a year.

Make your notebook personal—just between you and God. This week's Scripture memory passage tells you to ask, seek, and knock—in other words, keep searching!

FIVE HELPS IN DOING BIBLE STUDY

Day 1
Understanding the Words of the Bible

Read and mark *Matthew 7:7* in your Bible. Use your Scripture memory passage card to begin memorizing this verse.

The Bible we use today is easy to read and understand, because it has been translated into English. Fortunately, there are many good English translations and paraphrases. Originally, however, the Bible was written in three languages.

Can you name these original languages?
1. _____
2. _____
3. _____

Most of the Old Testament was written in Hebrew, with some portions in Aramaic. Greek was the original language of the New Testament. Because some words in these languages don't have exact equivalents in English, it helps to understand the original language in studying the Bible. So, how fluent are you in Greek? Not so great?! OK, because most of us aren't language scholars, we use English Bible translations and Bible study tools to help us understand the language.

On the drawing of the hand write "Five Helps in Doing Bible Study" on the little finger.

The first help is understanding the importance of the words of the Bible. These guidelines will help you with Bible words.

FOUR GUIDELINES ABOUT WORD STUDIES
Guideline 1—Decide if the word you are studying is broad or narrow in meaning. A narrow word has a limited meaning and usage. A broad word has a variety of meanings, making it more difficult to define. To determine this, see if the word deals with a large theme of the Bible (like *love*) or a specific theme (like *altar*).

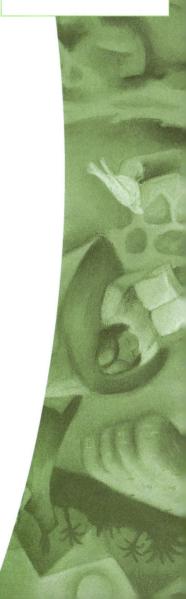

A STUDENT'S GUIDE TO STUDYING THE BIBLE

Read *1 Peter 2:9.* Select three words in this verse that would probably be difficult to study because of the broad meanings of the words. (See the suggested answers at the end of today's study.)

_____ _____ _____

Guideline 2—*Discover the meaning of the word as it is used in the Bible.* A Bible dictionary, study Bible or concordance can help you define Bible words.

Look up the word *sing* in a biblical concordance. Check out several verses associated with this word. How is *sing* used in the Bible? _____
_____

Guideline 3—*Study the word in the context where it appears.* Context often suggests the best meaning of a word. In our language the word *saint* refers to one who lives a holy, good life. In the New Testament *saint* appears in several of Paul's introductions in his letters.

Look at *Ephesians 1:1* and *Philippians 1:1.* Whom did Paul call *saints?*
_____

To Paul all Christians in the church were saints, because they were set apart to do God's will. *Saint* means "set apart."

Guideline 4—*Broaden your study of Bible words with other methods of Bible study.* Don't let word studies be your only Bible study method. The word study method focuses on the small details of word meanings. Use other methods, such as Big-Picture Bible Study or Character Trait Bible Study, for example, to gain a full picture of what God is saying.

SIX STEPS FOR DOING A WORD STUDY
Step 1—*Select the word to study.* For your first few studies select a word with a narrow meaning.

On the last night of His life, Jesus prayed for His disciples, as well as for you and me. Read *John 17:17-19.* What word in these verses could you study?_____ (I hope you chose *sanctify!*)

Step 2—*Define the word.* Look up and write a definition from an English dictionary. Include synonyms and antonyms.

Dictionary definition: _____
_____

Synonyms: _____

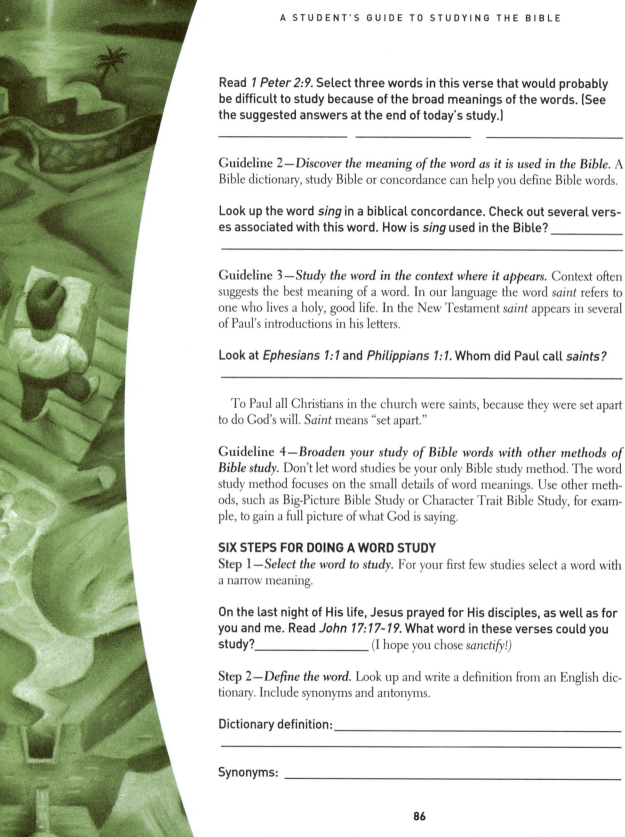

FIVE HELPS IN DOING BIBLE STUDY

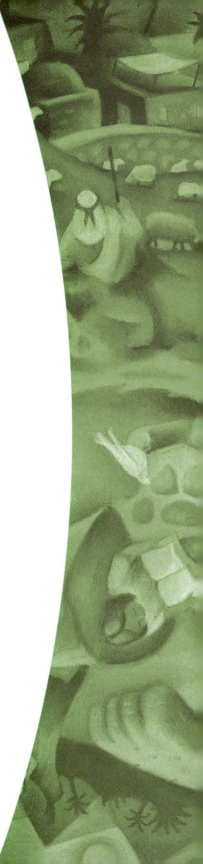

Antonyms: _____
_____

Step 3—*Discover Bible usages.* Use a Bible concordance to find other passages in the Bible where the selected word is used.

List three references for *sanctification* or *sanctify*.
1. _____
2. _____
3. _____

Step 4—*Identify the Bible meaning.* Write a definition of how the word is used in the Bible.

Define *sanctify* as used in *1 Corinthians 1:2*. _____
_____
_____
_____

Step 5—*Summarize what you have learned.* The summary may be an outline of Bible teachings about the word, or it may be a paragraph explaining the word. The summary prepares you to apply the word to your life.

Summarize *sanctification* here. _____
_____
_____
_____

Step 6—*Make application.* Finally, apply the Bible study to the four major areas of your life.

How can sanctification influence...
your relationship with God? _____
_____

your understanding of yourself? _____
_____

your relationship with others? _____
_____

your relationship with your church? _____
_____

(Suggested answers from *1 Peter 2:9: people, priesthood, nation.*)

A STUDENT'S GUIDE TO STUDYING THE BIBLE

Day 2
Understanding the Images of the Bible

A *metaphor* is a simple comparison, where one thing represents another.

A *simile* compares two unlike things using the words *like* or *as* in the comparison.

The Bible uses figures of speech to explain biblical truths. Figures of speech create word pictures and images to express the difficult and deep. A figure of speech can make an ordinary statement memorable by turning on the imagination. Biblical figures of speech normally came from the everyday life of the writer who believed the hearer or reader also understood the symbolic reference. For example, Paul called himself and Timothy "bondservants of Christ Jesus." Slavery was a part of Paul's New Testament world, although neither he nor Timothy were slaves. There are six figures of speech—metaphors, similes, personifications, understatements, overstatements, and rhetorical questions.

A *metaphor* is a simple comparison, where one thing represents another.

Jesus used two metaphors in *Matthew 5:13-14* to describe His followers. He called them _____ and _____ .

A *simile* compares two unlike things using the words *like* or *as* in the comparison.

Read *James 1:6*. What is the simile? _____
How is a doubting Christian like a wave in a rough ocean? _____
_____
_____
_____

Paul used similes in *1 Thessalonians 2:7,11*. They are:
verse 7 _____
_____

verse 11 _____
_____
_____

FIVE HELPS IN DOING BIBLE STUDY

A third type of imagery is *personification,* where a lifeless object receives life. For example, the writer might give human qualities to a nonhuman item, such as a tree.

Identify the personification in *James 5:4* and explain in your own words the idea James was trying to communicate. _____
_____
_____

Another figure of speech is **understatement.** Understatement helps a writer avoid a blunt or distasteful thought in a sentence.

How did Peter use understatement in *Acts 1:24-25* to avoid judgmental words about Judas' betrayal? _____
_____
_____

Understatement also can use a negative statement to state a positive truth.

How did the understatement in *Galatians 5:22-23* compare the power of the Holy Spirit in a Christian's life to the power of law enforcement? ___
_____
_____

The fifth type of imagery is the opposite of understatement; it's *overstatement.* There are three types of overstatement. The first is an intentional exaggeration to communicate a truth, called a *hyperbole.* Jesus used overstatement in *Matthew 5:30.*

What was Jesus exaggerating in this overstatement? Why did Jesus' use hyperbole? _____
_____
_____

A second form of overstatement combines ideas that are opposites such as "thunderous silence." This is called an *oxymoron.*

What two opposites did Paul use to describe the Macedonian Christians in *2 Corinthians 8:2?* _____

Irony is a third form of overstatement. In this figure of speech, the words are the opposite of the writer's true feelings. If you jump into icy water, and someone asks, "How's the water?", and you reply "Fine!" through clenched chattering teeth, that's irony.

A STUDENT'S GUIDE TO STUDYING THE BIBLE

What was ironic about the Roman soldiers' taunts to Jesus in *Matthew 27:29?* _____
_____
_____

The final figure of speech today is the ***rhetorical question.*** The writer or speaker asks this question for effect and emphasis. Since the answer is obvious, no answer is expected.

Several rhetorical questions are expressed in *Romans 6:1-3.* Why did Paul ask these questions? _____
_____
_____

To be sure you understand imagery, match each figure of speech and its definition to the Scripture example. You will find the answers in tomorrow's Bible study.
 ___1. Metaphor: Compares one object to another without using *like* or *as.*
 ___2. Simile: Compares one object to another using *like* or *as.*
 ___3. Personification: Suggests a lifeless object has life.
 ___4. Understatement: Uses to avoid a blunt or distasteful thought in a sentence or as a negative statement to declare a positive truth.
 ___5. Overstatement—hyperbole: Intentionally exaggerates a point.
 ___6. Overstatement—oxymoron: Combines ideas that are opposites.
 ___7. Overstatement—irony: Expresses the opposite of what a person feels.
 ___8. Rhetorical question: Asks a question where the answer is obvious.

a. *1 Thessalonians 4:14*
b. *2 Corinthians 8:2*
c. *Psalm 114:5-6*
d. *John 21:25*
e. *James 4:14*
f. *1 Thessalonians 2:11*
g. *James 3:6*
h. *Matthew 27:29*

Don't forget to work on this week's Scripture memory passage *Matthew 7:7.*

FIVE HELPS IN DOING BIBLE STUDY

Day 3
Understanding the Grammar of the Bible

> The answers to yesterday's study on figures of speech are: 1g, 2f, 3c, 4a, 5d, 6b, 7h, 8e.

Understanding the grammar of the Bible is the third help in deciphering the Bible. No, this isn't a lesson on English grammar. Basic grammar, however, opens up your Bible study. A grammatical study by itself may not be very interesting, so combine it with other types of study, such as Big-Picture Bible Study or Close-Up Bible Study.

STATEMENTS
Look at the four kinds of statements found in the Bible.
- Fact
- Promise
- Warning
- Command

Statements of *fact* are found most often in the history books of the Bible. Review week 3, day 1 to identify these history books. Some statements of fact deal with events. Other statements of fact deal with theological truths.

What fact does *Acts 2:41* express? _____
_____
_____
_____

Statements of *warning* express alarm over something to avoid. Bible words and phrases like *beware* or *take heed* or *be careful* or *watch out* introduce a warning.

What is the warning in *Luke 12:15?* _____
_____
_____
_____

Statements of *promise* confirm something will happen. Some promises come with conditions. If you do a certain thing, you will receive the promise.

A STUDENT'S GUIDE TO STUDYING THE BIBLE

What is the promise in this week's Scripture memory passage? *(Matt. 7:7)* What are the conditions? _____
_____
_____

Statements of *command* call to action, while warning statements sound an alarm. Command statements often come with obligations.

What commands are in *John 13:34-35?* What is the obligation? _____
_____
_____
_____

What kind of statement is each week's Scripture memory passage?
First Corinthians 2:14 is a statement of _____.
First Peter 5:6-7 is a statement of _____.
James 4:4 is a statement of _____.
James 1:2-4 is a statement of _____.

CONNECTIVES WORDS
Conjunctions and prepositions join parts of sentences. *Because* is the connective word in the statement, "I didn't come to your party because I was sick."

Some connective words like *after*, *before*, *when*, or *while* show **time**. Sometimes the time relationship helps you understand what's happening.

What is the connective word in *Matthew 26:32?* How does the word establish a time relationship? _____
_____
_____

Other connective words show the **reason** behind certain actions. *Because*, *that*, and *for* show the relationship between cause and effect, emphasizing the cause.

Identify the connective word in *John 10:10b.* What is the cause and effect? _____
_____
_____
_____

Some connectives **introduce** or show **results**. *For*, *thus*, *then*, and *also* show the relationship between cause and effect, but *this* emphasizes the effect. Someone has said that whenever you see the word *therefore* in the Bible, you need to figure out what it's "there for."

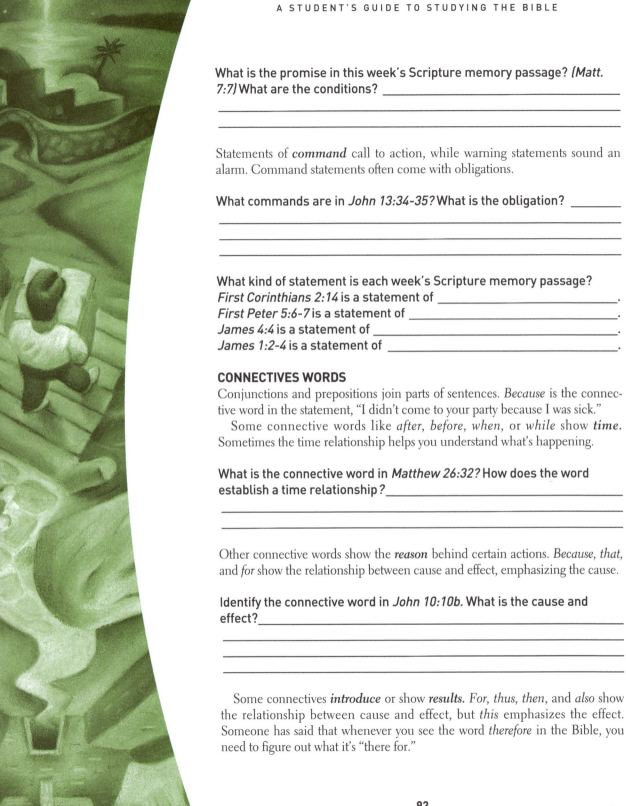

Identify the connective word in *2 Thessalonians 2:14-15*. What is the cause and effect? _____
_____
_____
_____

The final group of connectives shows *purpose*. The connectives *so that, in order that,* and *because* indicate relationship between action and purpose.

Identify the connective word in *1 John 5:13*. What is the action and purpose? _____
_____
_____

PARTS OF SPEECH

Although there are eight parts of speech, you will study only five—verb, noun, pronoun, adjective, and adverb.

A *verb* shows action or existence. Verbs also have tense, meaning they show time relationships. Verb tenses are present (an event happening now), past (an event from the past), and future (an event that has not happened). Observing the tense of a verb helps you understand and apply the meaning of a statement.

Here's an example of how important verb tense can be in understanding the Bible. Check the statement that expresses your idea of salvation.
❏ You were saved when you repented of your sin and accepted Jesus.
❏ You are being saved daily.
❏ Your salvation will take place in the future after death.

You answered correctly if you checked all three! Read *Philippians 1:6* in your Bible. The verb tenses teach that salvation has already taken place, is now taking place, and will take place in the future.

Write the related phrases from *Philippians 1:6* beside each statement.
You were saved . . . _____
You are being saved . . . _____
Your salvation will take place . . . _____

Verbs have an *active* and a *passive* voice. Active voice shows the subject acting or carrying out the action. Passive voice shows the subject receiving the action.

Identify each verse as either active or passive.
Ephesians 2:8 ❏ active ❏ passive
Matthew 4:20 ❏ active ❏ passive

Why did you identify each verse the way you did? _____
_____
_____

A *noun* names a person, place, or thing. A proper noun is the name of a particular person, place, or thing. In the Bible names often describe the spiritual possibilities of a person. For example, Peter means "rock." Some proper nouns identify places where something significant occurred. For example, Decapolis in *Mark 7:31* in Greek means "ten cities." Most of the ten towns lay east of the Jordan River.

Pronouns replace nouns. The word for which the pronoun stands is called its antecedent.

What is the pronoun in *Acts 8:4*? _____ **Now find the antecedent by looking at verses prior to *verse 4*. What is the antecedent?** _____
What verse is it in? _____

Adjectives modify nouns and pronouns.

What adjective did Peter use in *1 Peter 1:22* to describe Christian love?
_____

Adverbs modify verbs, adjectives, and other adverbs.

What adverb did Paul use in *Titus 3:6* to describe how God pours out His Spirit on a Christian?
_____

So far this week, you've studied three of the five helps in doing Bible study. They are:
1. Understanding the w_____ of the Bible
2. Understanding the i_____ of the Bible
3. Understanding the g_____ of the Bible

FIVE HELPS IN DOING BIBLE STUDY

Day 4
Understanding the Topics of the Bible

The fourth help in doing Bible study is to understand the topics of the Bible. A topical Bible study looks at various subjects in the Bible. It provides a logical, orderly method of studying the Bible. It offers a balanced understanding of the Bible's teaching on a particular subject.

- Study one topic in a single book of the Bible. For example, you could study the teachings on the use of the tongue in James.
- Trace a topic throughout Scripture. Study the miracles of the Bible, for example.
- The topic can be narrow, such as prophecies about Jesus' birth, or broad, such as all biblical prophecies.
- Look at doctrinal topics, such as the nature of God or the work of the Holy Spirit. Or, choose practical topics, such as ministries in a local church.
- Use a topical study to gather and organize the guidelines and instructions on what the Bible teaches about the use of time, money, or marriage.
- Some Bibles and study guides already contain a list of topics with the related Scripture references. Does your Bible have a page of topics with biblical references to study?

TOPICAL BIBLE STUDY STEPS

These steps are similar to the Character Trait Bible Study method you studied in week 5.

Step 1—*Select a topic.* Select a topic you have a spiritual interest in or where you need more information. For some subjects, limit your research to one Bible book. What topics in the Bible would you like to study?

For today's study, let's do a topical study on "the tongue." Since this can be a broad topic, choose either the book of *Proverbs* or the book of *James* to find teachings about the tongue.

Scripture References: ____

_____
_____
_____
_____
_____
_____
_____
_____
_____
_____
_____
_____
_____

Outline: _____

_____
_____
_____
_____
_____
_____
_____
_____
_____
_____
_____
_____
_____
_____
_____
_____
_____
_____

Step 2—*List related words.* Write down synonyms, phrases, or ideas that have something in common with your topic. If you are studying "the tongue," related words might include *speaking, talking, language, cursing, blessing, words, slang,* or *argue.* Look up *tongue* in a topical concordance.

List related words from the concordance. _____
_____

Step 3—*Study the verses.* Record verses that relate to your specific topic of study. For today's study focus on verses in either *Proverbs* or *James* related to the moral teachings about using the tongue.

List several Scripture references and key thoughts in the margin. (If you use a computer program to search for topics, your program may give you either the biblical references or the specific verse. Eliminate verses you don't need and print out the listing.)

Step 4—*Write an observation, comment, or question for each reference.* Include questions about issues you don't understand.

Write your comments and questions about two verses you found for the tongue. _____
_____

Step 5—*Organize the verses.* As you gather references, notice which verses relate to specific parts of your topic. In studying the topic of the tongue, for example, you will find verses about good uses of the tongue, bad uses of the tongue, controlling the tongue, and God's judgment of the tongue. Use another sheet of paper to organize these verses into subtopics.

Step 6—*Make an outline.* Once the references are grouped together, arrange them into an outline. Name several subdivisions under a main topic. Each subdivision should contain a list of the verses related to that point.

Make a brief outline in the margin, or if you need more space, use a separate sheet of paper.

Step 7—*Write a summary.* Conclude your study by summarizing your outline. The outline provides you with a complete view of what you have studied. The summary condenses what you've learned into a few words. Your conclusion should contain not only a summary of teachings, but also ideas for personal or relational application. Do this on a sheet of paper.

There! You've completed your first topical Bible study.

FIVE HELPS IN DOING BIBLE STUDY

Day Five
Understanding the Doctrines of the Bible

Take a quick quiz. Write True or False beside each statement. You will discover the answers in today's study.
_____ 1. Bible truths are easy to understand because they are presented in a systematic, organized way.
_____ 2. Some truths can be discovered by reading the Bible carefully.
_____ 3. Bible writers assume nothing; they tell us everything.
_____ 4. No section of the Bible is completely theological in content.

The fifth help for doing Bible study is Doctrinal Bible Study. A doctrinal study looks at what the Bible teaches or assumes about such topics as God, Christ, the Holy Spirit, humanity, salvation, and the church. The Bible is not organized by topics or doctrines. Its teachings about God and Christ appear throughout the Bible. (Number 1 is false.) Doctrinal Bible Study helps us fit together what the Bible says about God's truths. Doctrinal study falls into at least three types.

Assumptions—Biblical writers make numerous assumptions about the doctrine of God. (Statement number 3 is false.) For example, biblical writers accept the existence of God. They do not argue for it or seek to prove it. God exists. You can discover numerous assumptions by carefully reading a book of the Bible. (Number 2 is true.)

What did the writer of *1 Thessalonians 5:2* assume? _____
_____

Sometimes a writer indicates an assumption by using the phrase "we know." Paraphrase Paul's assumption in *2 Corinthians 5:1.* _____
_____
_____

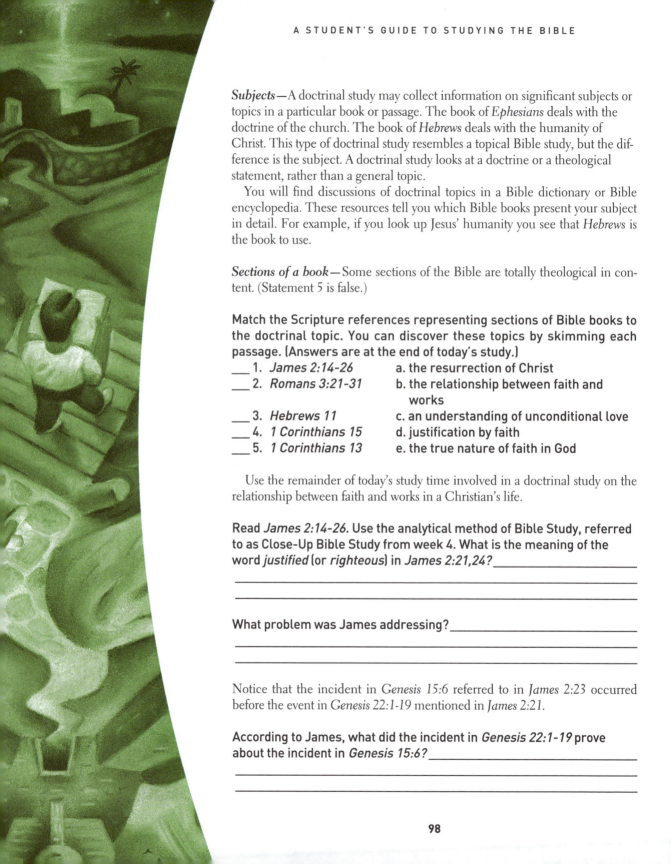

Subjects—A doctrinal study may collect information on significant subjects or topics in a particular book or passage. The book of *Ephesians* deals with the doctrine of the church. The book of *Hebrews* deals with the humanity of Christ. This type of doctrinal study resembles a topical Bible study, but the difference is the subject. A doctrinal study looks at a doctrine or a theological statement, rather than a general topic.

You will find discussions of doctrinal topics in a Bible dictionary or Bible encyclopedia. These resources tell you which Bible books present your subject in detail. For example, if you look up Jesus' humanity you see that *Hebrews* is the book to use.

Sections of a book—Some sections of the Bible are totally theological in content. (Statement 5 is false.)

Match the Scripture references representing sections of Bible books to the doctrinal topic. You can discover these topics by skimming each passage. (Answers are at the end of today's study.)
___ 1. *James 2:14-26*   a. the resurrection of Christ
___ 2. *Romans 3:21-31*   b. the relationship between faith and works
___ 3. *Hebrews 11*   c. an understanding of unconditional love
___ 4. *1 Corinthians 15*   d. justification by faith
___ 5. *1 Corinthians 13*   e. the true nature of faith in God

Use the remainder of today's study time involved in a doctrinal study on the relationship between faith and works in a Christian's life.

Read *James 2:14-26*. Use the analytical method of Bible Study, referred to as Close-Up Bible Study from week 4. What is the meaning of the word *justified* (or *righteous*) in *James 2:21,24*? _____
_____
_____

What problem was James addressing? _____
_____
_____

Notice that the incident in *Genesis 15:6* referred to in *James 2:23* occurred before the event in *Genesis 22:1-19* mentioned in *James 2:21*.

According to James, what did the incident in *Genesis 22:1-19* prove about the incident in *Genesis 15:6*? _____
_____
_____

FIVE HELPS IN DOING BIBLE STUDY

How was Rahab justified by her deeds according to *Joshua 2.* _____
_____
_____

What did James give as evidence of a dead faith in *James 2:14-20?* ____
_____
_____

What results did James suggest for genuine faith in *James 2:21-26?* ___
_____
_____
_____

Summarize what *James 2:14-26* teaches. _____
_____
_____
_____
_____

How would you apply James' teaching to your own life? _____
_____
_____
_____
_____

To get a balanced view of a particular doctrine study several passages on that doctrine. Get a balanced view of the relationship between faith and works by checking out *Romans 3:21-31*; *Galatians 2:17-21*; and *Ephesians 2:8-10.*

How do these sections fit with what you learned in James? _____
_____
_____
_____
_____

You made it! Hooray! Congratulations! Well-Done! You have completed a six-week course of how to study and understand the Bible. You faithfully stuck to the commitment you made in the Introduction. (Look back to see if you were able to "get with the plan.")

Now for a final review of what you've studied over the past six weeks.

Thumb: One P_____: A S_____ H_____
First Finger: Two R_____ to G_____ Bible Study

A STUDENT'S GUIDE TO STUDYING THE BIBLE

First Finger: Two R_____ to G_____ Bible Study
Rule 1: I_____ the Bible C_____.
Identify the T_____ of W_____.
N_____ the Context.
T_____ the Bible to I_____ Itself.
E_____ the Writer's M_____.
Remember the L_____ of R_____.

Rule 2: A _____ the Bible W_____.
Ask W_____ the Verse Means.
P_____ the Bible as a Book of S_____.
P_____ __ the P_____ Carefully.
L_____ about the C_____.
Y_____ must U_____ the Technique of O_____.

Middle Finger: Three W_____ to D____ Bible Study
First Way: B____-P_____ Bible Study
Second Way: C_____-U_____ Bible Study
Third Way: B_____ Bible Study

Ring Finger: Four A_____ to A_____ Bible Study
Your Relationship to _____
Your Understanding of Y_____
Your Relationship with _____
Your Relationship with the _____

Little Finger: Five H_____ in Doing Bible Study
Understanding the W_____ of the Bible
Understanding the I_____ of the Bible
Understanding the G_____ of the Bible
Understanding the T_____ of the Bible
Understanding the D_____ of the Bible

God's great blessings on you as you continue to let God's Word
    teach you
        inspire you
            transform you.
                      Amen.

(Answers to doctrinal study match-ups: 1b, 2d, 3e, 4a, 5c.)

GROUP LEARNING ACTIVITIES

Introductory Group Session

Plan a brief session to give out books and to introduce the six-week study. Here is a suggested agenda for this introductory session.

- Hand out copies of *A Student's Guide to Studying the Bible*.
- Review the Introduction on page 5.
- Ask students to share what they expect to learn from this study.
- Lead students to draw a hand in the front of their books.
- Direct students to the Scripture memory cards on pages 109-110. Show them how to use each week's card. Review ways to memorize Scripture.
- Invite students to sign their books on page 5 as a commitment to the six-week study.
- Suggest students pair off to form accountability partners. Or, set up a chat room on the Internet to meet and challenge one another. Point out that each week in the group session, students will review their work and discuss ways to put what they've learned into practice.
- Pray for God's guidance in understanding His Word and strength to stay faithful to the task.

Session 1
Are You Ready?

GOALS FOR THIS SESSION
As students evaluate week 1 involve them in ...
- putting their commitment to the Bible study into action,
- reviewing the Scripture memory passage,
- using tools to aid Bible study.

BEFORE THE SESSION
- *Step 1*–Draw a hand print on a large sheet of paper. Bring this visual to each group session.
- *Step 2*–Write the Scripture memory passage on three-by-five inch cards, one word per card.
- *Step 3*–Bring several Bible translations.
- *Step 4*—Bring available Bible study aids.

DURING THE SESSION
Step 1 Weekly Review (10 min.)
As students arrive, informally ask them how their first week's daily study time went. Ask: **How did you feel about each day's study? What time worked best for your daily study? What day of the study was the most helpful? Why? What barriers or distractions threatened to keep you from your daily study? How did you handle these? What might you do next week to improve your daily study time?**

Step 2 Memory Madness (10 min.)
Continue the discussion by asking **How did you feel about this week's Scripture memory passage? What technique helped you memorize this week's verses?**

Randomly scatter the previously prepared Scripture memory passage three-by-five inch cards on the floor or a table. Tell students to arrange the cards to quote week 1's Scripture memory passage. Repeat the verse as a group. Remove cards that contain nouns, and repeat the verse aloud. Remove cards that contain verbs, and repeat the verse. Continue removing words until the students are repeating the verse without relying on the cards.

Step 3 Translation Inspection (10 min.)
Ask students to identify the Bible translations they are using. Ask: **What is the difference between a Bible translation and a paraphrase of the Bible?** Assign students to read aloud and compare one or two familiar Bible passages *(Rom. 12:1-2* or *Matt. 5:3-10)* from several translations and paraphrases. If you have *A Har-*

mony of the Synoptic Gospels, show students how it presents the temptation of Jesus.

Step 4 Tool Time (25 min.)
Ask students to look at week 1, day 4 and share many of the Bible study helps they have in their Bibles or in their homes. Show an example of each Bible study help (Bible dictionary, commentary, atlas, topical Bible, concordance, and encyclopedia), if possible. Be sure students understand how to use each tool.

Direct students to week 1, day 5. Go through the list of questions, letting students call out which Bible study tools could help locate answers to each question. (For example, by Barak they may put "d" for Bible dictionary. For *1 Corinthians* 8 they may list "a," "b," and "g" for modern translation, paraphrased translation, and Bible commentary.)

Invite students to work with a friend and answer two or three of the questions using the Bible study tools. Offer help when needed. Call for the answers that students found.

Step 5 Closing Concerns (5 min.)
Repeat this week's Scripture memory passage. Challenge students to be faithful in week 2. Let accountability partners get together and pray. Or, pray for individual students' concerns and the coming week of study as a group.

Session 2
One Bible Study Prerequisite

GOALS FOR THIS SESSION
As students evaluate week 2, involve them in . . .
- examining the need for spiritual hunger when doing Bible study,
- expressing what's involved in spiritual hunger,
- looking at this week's Scripture memory passage,
- discussing personal concerns of their studies.

BEFORE THE SESSION
- ❏ *Step 1*–On the way to this session, stop and get an order of French fries from a fast food place. Or, bring a popcorn popper, popcorn, a bowl, butter, and salt. Bring the hand visual from session 1.
- ❏ *Step 2*–Provide large sheets of paper, markers, yarn, scissors, and masking tape.
- ❏ *Step 3*–Write the incorrect version of this week's Scripture memory passage on a chalkboard or poster. (See page 103.)

DURING THE SESSION
Step 1 Hungry Makers (10 min.)
Place the freshly fried French fries close to the door, so students smell them as they arrive. Or, if you use popcorn, pop a batch for students to munch on as everyone arrives. Ask: **When you are really hungry what do you like to eat? How does being hungry for something make it difficult to pay attention to other things?** Finally, invite students to share a time when they were really hungry.

Write on the thumb of the hand visual from group session 1 One Prerequisite. Ask: **What prerequisite is vital to making Bible study effective? How would you define spiritual hunger based on this week's study? Can a person be spiritually hungry and not be a Christian?** (Yes, that is one way God draws people to Him. God makes them "hungry" to know Him.) **How can having a spiritual hunger help you study the Bible?**

Say: **One thing you studied this week involved your relationship with God through believing in Jesus Christ.** Take time to review how a person becomes a Christian by sharing the following:
- All people are sinners in need of God's love and salvation. Read *Romans 3:23; 6:23.*
- But, God has a plan to restore the relationship between God and a sinner. Read *Romans 5:8.*
- **That plan begins with a person repenting from sin and putting their faith in Jesus Christ as a personal friend, guide, and Savior.** Read *Romans 10:9* and *Philippians 2:9-11.*

Say: **If you want to know more about this personal relationship with God, I'll be glad to talk with you after the session or at any time.**

Step 2 Hungry Helpers (30 min.)
Direct students to turn to week 2, day 4. Invite volunteers to share their responses to the agree/disagree statements at the beginning of that day's study. Discuss statement 4. Remind students that God can speak to them personally and directly through the Scripture. God also provides helps for understanding the Bible.

Divide students into five teams. (If you have a small group, one person can work on an assignment.) Assign each team a day from this week's Bible study. Direct teams to develop a promotion that informs other students how to meet that spiritual hunger. (For example, the day 1 team could present the necessary relationship; the day 2 team could work on the reason; day 3, attitude; day 4, the Holy Spirit; day 5, discipline.) Suggest teams choose to design a poster, prepare a skit, produce a TV or radio news story, or write a jingle promoting their day's information. Point out the basic art supplies. Call for each team's informative presentation.

Direct students to turn to the agree/disagree statements in week 2, day 5 on page 34. Call on volunteers to share how they answered the five statements. Ask, **How can the "No pain, no gain" statement apply to studying the Bible?** Call on students to read *2 Timothy 2:15* aloud from several different translations.

Step 3 Memory Madness (10 min.)
Invite students to share how this week's memory work went. Display the poster on which you have written (or write on the chalkboard) the following incorrect version of *1 Corinthians 2:14*. (The mistakes are underlined, but do not underline them on the poster or chalkboard.)

The _human_ without the _right attitude_ does not accept the _blessings_ that come from the spirit of _faith_, for they are _inappropriate_ to him, and he cannot understand them, because they are _physically felt_.

Challenge students to correct the incorrect words or phrases. Ask, **What does spiritually discerned mean?** Invite them to share shortcuts they've learned in memorizing Scripture. Direct students to get with their accountability partners and recite both week's Scripture memory passages.

Step 4 Closing Concerns (10 min.)
Tell students to share concerns about their daily work with their accountability partners. Suggest accountability partners say something encouraging to one another. Close with prayer.

Session 3
Two Rules to Guide Bible Study

GOALS FOR THIS SESSION
As students evaluate week 3, involve them in . . .
- reviewing the rules of interpreting and applying the Bible,
- deciding which rules apply to specific Scripture,
- discussing completed charts and activities,
- continuing to work on Scripture memory passages,
- praying for one another.

BEFORE THE SESSION
- ❏ *Step 1*—Hang a large sheet of paper on a focal wall or place it on a table. Label this paper *Rules of the House*. Bring markers. Bring the hand visual from group session 1.
- ❏ *Step 2*—Prepare the game using three-by-five inch cards and markers.
- ❏ *Step 3*—Write the Scripture references without the information in parentheses on slips of paper. Bring Bible dictionaries and commentaries.

DURING THE SESSION
Step 1 Rules of the House (5 min.)
As students arrive direct them to the large sheet of paper on which you've written *Rules of the House*. Hand out markers and tell students to write in graffiti-

fashion the rules at their houses. (For example, "I take out the trash on Tuesdays"; "Only the dirty clothes in the hamper will be washed.") Review students' rules. Explain that students have been studying Two Rules to Guide Bible Study this week. Write this on the hand visual. Call on students to state the two rules (Interpret the Bible Correctly and Apply the Bible Wisely).

Step 2 Concentrate! (15 min.)
To test students on these rules, divide them into two teams. Place the 20 three-by-five inch cards on the floor, numbered side up. (Prepare the cards by writing the first word of each guideline on a three-by-five inch card and the rest of the phrase on a second three-by-five inch card. For example, write "Identify" on one card and "the type of writing" on the second card. When all 20 cards are done, turn them over, shuffle them and number the backs of the cards from 1 to 20.) Play the game, matching the first word of the Bible study guideline with the second part of the guideline. At the end of the game, place the matches on the floor or a focal wall where everyone can see them.

Step 3 Practical Practicing (15 min.)
Ask: **How did you feel about the five guidelines for interpreting the Bible correctly? How did you feel about the five guidelines for applying the Bible wisely?**

Explain that during the week students looked up verses to support each guideline. Say: **I'm going to hand out Scripture passages. After reading these in your Bible, decide which guidelines to use in understanding your verse.** (Suggested applicable guidelines are in parentheses. Do not include this information on students' slips.)
- *Isaiah 1:15-16* (identify writing; ask meaning; overstatement)
- *Matthew 6:1-7* (context)
- *Matthew 21:22* and *James 4:3* (interpret itself; ask meaning)
- *Titus 2:11-13* and *1 Thessalonians 4:13-18* (limits of revelation)
- *Ephesians 4:26* (ask meaning)
- *Acts 2:42-45* (type of writing, book of standards)
- *1 Corinthians 8:13* (context, standards, culture)
- *Luke 2:25-26* (promises)
- *2 Corinthians 13:12* (culture)
- *Matthew 5:29* (overstatement)

Allow students to refer to their workbooks for help. Briefly discuss how each guideline can help a Bible student.

Step 4 Chart Checking (10 min.)
Review two charts that students completed during the week. Look at the chart from week 3, day 3 that deals with meaning and applications. Have students share what they thought the verses meant. Call on volunteers to share applications for each Scripture. Next, look at the promises chart at the end of week 3, day 4. Ask students to share what type of promises each Scripture contained.

Step 5 Memory Madness (10 min.)
Invite volunteers to say the Scripture memory passages for week 1 *(Ps. 19:7-8)* and week 2 *(1 Cor. 2:14)*. To help everyone remember this week's verse *(1 Pet. 5:6-7)*, work as a group to make up hand and body motions of the Scripture. Repeat the verse several times using the hand motions. Continue to repeat the verse, verbally dropping phrases, but continuing with the hand and body motions. Do this until students are silently making the motions in unison.

Step 6 Closing Concerns (5 min.)
Direct everyone to get with their accountability partners. Suggest partners share how their week of study went. Remind them to pray for one another.

Session 4
Three Ways to Do Bible Study

GOALS FOR THIS SESSION
As students evaluate week 4, involve them in . . .
- expressing an understanding of the three ways to do Bible study,
- sharing examples of each of the ways,
- reviewing this week's Scripture memory passage,
- praying with a guided prayer.

BEFORE THE SESSION
- ❑ *Step 1*—Display the hand visual used in previous sessions.
- ❑ *Step 2*—Review the different methods of Bible presented in week 4.
- ❑ *Step 3*—Write each word of *Philippians* 4:6-7 on separate slips of paper. Make two or more sets based on group size. Place each set in separate brown paper bags. Shake up the bags. Bring masking tape.

DURING THE SESSION
Step 1 City Slickers (10 min.)
Direct students to turn to the opening activity of week 4, day 1. Ask which boxes they checked under each statement. Ask: **How does flying over a city give you the big picture? What could you learn about a city just by flying over it?** (size, sports interests from types of ball fields, growth potential, landmarks around a city) **How does walking around a city and talking with citizens give you the close-up picture? What might you learn about a city just by walking around it?** (friendliness of the people, types of shops and restaurants, where people hang out, the language of a city, the amount of traffic) **What might you learn about a city from your research?** (actual growth, who owns what land, crops or industry, history of city)

Say: **This is what you've been studying this week—studying the Bible by looking at the big picture, studying the Bible by looking at it close up,** and by using background Bible study.

Have students identify what this week's topic was. Write *Three Ways to Do Bible Study* on the middle finger of the hand visual.

Step 2 The Big Three (30 min.)
To be sure students understand the differences between these three methods of Bible study, direct them to turn to the last activity of week 4, day 1. Ask students to defend their choices (Big-Picture method, the Close-Up method, or the Background method) for each Scripture. Although the copy suggests which best fit, challenge students to defend their choices.

To evaluate the Big-Picture method, work as a group through the Bible study in week 4, day 2. Ask students to read some of their responses to the questions about *Philemon* on page 56 and the chart of *Philemon* on page 57.

To evaluate the Close-Up Bible study method, look at week 4, day 3. Call on volunteers to share their paraphrases of *Philippians* 4:6-7. Ask other students to share their observations about *Philippians* 4:4-7. Call on others to share the questions they wrote down. Invite students to share their summaries or outlines. Let students share their writings from week 4, day 3. Focus on examples that compare *Philippians* 4:4-7 with related Scripture. Direct students to share how they could personalize this study.

To evaluate the Background Bible Study method, look at week 4, day 5. Invite students to share responses to the Bible studies under History, Geography, Culture, and Sociology. Encourage questions about methods they don't understand.

Step 3 Memory Madness (10 min.)
Ask students how they feel about their Scripture memory passages each week. Divide students into two teams. Give each team a paper bag containing the slips of paper on which you've written the words for this week's Scripture memory passage. Tell each team member to pull out a word from the bag and put the words in the right order. (If you work with younger youth, make this a relay race. Put each bag and masking tape across the room from each team. Tell team

members to run down one by one, pull out a word, and tape it in the correct order on the wall.) After the relay is completed, lead volunteers to say all four Scripture memory passages aloud.

Step 4 Closing Concerns (10 min.)
After accountability partners have met for a few minutes, lead everyone in a guided prayer. Base your prayer statements on this week's Scripture memory passage *Philippians 4:6-7*. For example, you might say: *Pray for something that makes you anxious. Offer thanksgiving to God for something good in your life. Thank God for the ability to seek Him in prayer. Thank God for His peace. Ask God to keep you safe and to guard your heart. Thank God for Jesus Christ. Amen.*

Session 5
Four Areas to Apply Bible Study

GOALS FOR THIS SESSION
As students evaluate week 5, involve them in . . .
- determining a Bible personality they want to be,
- reviewing the four areas of application,
- applying Bible study to each area of application,
- picking a trait to apply to their lives.

BEFORE THE SESSION
❏ *Step 1*—Display the hand visual used in previous sessions.
❏ *Step 2*—Review the four areas of biblical application presented in week 5.
❏ *Step 3*—Prepare four assignments cards from the instructions in step 3. If you have a large group, make several sets of assignment cards, so that each team only has four or five students. Bring pencils, white paper, and a couple of hymnals.
❏ *Step 4*—Bring rocks that are big enough to write on, but small enough to be carried in a pocket. Bring permanent markers.

DURING THE SESSION
Step 1 What If . . . (10 min.)
On a chalkboard write *What if you could be any person in the world, who would you want to be?* As students arrive, point out the question and invite them to share their answers with one another. Call on volunteers to share who they would like to be and why. Ask: **What Bible person would you want to be? Why?** Suggest they thumb through a Bible if they need a few ideas. After several have shared, explain: **This week you looked at biblical application for four areas of life.** Write *Four Areas to Apply Bible Study* on the hand visual. Say: **While you may not be able to become someone else, you are learning how the Bible can be applied to your life to help you become the person God wants you to be. Let's review these four areas of application.**

Step 2 Applications Wanted (15 min.)
Divide students into four teams. Assign each team one area of application—relationship with God, understanding yourself, relationship with others, relationship with the church. Direct teams to review the definition of their assigned relationship by looking at week 5, day 1. Teams should be able to explain how the Bible can be applied to their assigned area of application. After a few minutes, call for team reports.

Step 3 Real Time Application (25 min.)
Using the same four teams and the same areas of application, make these assignments.
 The Relationship with God Team—Write a dialogue between John Mark and God based on the Biographical Bible Study of John Mark you did on week 5, day 2.
 The Understanding Yourself Team—Write a poem, rap, or journal entry using the Character Trait Bible study you did on week 5, day 3.
 The Relationship with Others Team—Use your Character Trait Bible study of Barnabas on week 5, day 5. Decide how the characteristics you studied apply to your relationship with family, school friends, and a coach or other adult. Make three frozen-statute arrangements that depict these relationships. (A frozen

statute arrangement involves each team member standing in a certain way to show the relationship with the main person.)

The Relationship with the Church Team—Use the Devotional study from Lamentations that you did on week 5, day 5. Select words and phrases that explain how these verses apply to your relationship with the church. Write new words to a favorite hymn explaining this relationship. Consider using the Doxology ("Praise God, From Whom All Blessings Flow").

Let teams work for 15 minutes. Then, call them together, letting each team share its presentation.

Step 4 Memory Madness (10 min.)
Encourage volunteers to lead others in saying this week's Scripture memory passage. Ask: **What are the character traits in these verses?** *(joy, maturity, perseverance, completeness)* **Which character trait do you believe you have? Which character trait would you like to develop?**

Hand each person a small rock and a permanent marker. Ask: **How are big rocks used? How are little rocks used? How can rocks build up something? How can rocks destroy something?**

Tell students to write the trait they have or desire on their rocks using the permanent markers. Challenge them to put their rocks where they can see them during the week. Suggest they look for ways to develop or enhance that trait in themselves during the week.

Recite the Scripture memory passage as a closing prayer.

Session 6
Five Helps in Doing Bible Study

GOALS FOR THIS SESSION
As students evaluate week 6, involve them in . . .
- reciting the six Scripture memory passages;
- presenting the five helps studied during the week;
- expressing their personal feelings about the six-week study;
- participating in a closing prayer experience.

BEFORE THE SESSION
❑ *Step 1*—Bring a set of Scripture memory passage cards, or write each week's Scripture memory passage on a separate three-by-five inch card.
❑ *Step 2*—Bring large and small construction paper, markers, string, scissors, and masking tape. Display the hand visual.
❑ *Step 3*—Bring several sheets of construction paper in a variety of colors. Cut the construction paper into three-inch strips.

DURING THE SESSION
Step 1 Memory Madness (15 min.)
Divide students into two teams. Play "Scripture Charades." Put the Scripture memory passage cards in a stack. Have teams take turns drawing a card and letting one person act out the Scripture memory passage. Continue until one team guesses the correct Scripture and repeats it correctly. If a team can't say the passage correctly, the other team gets to try. Play until all the Scripture memory passage cards have been used. Applaud students for working to memorize Scripture during these six weeks. Discuss ways to continue to memorize Scripture. Ask: **What methods helped you memorize Scripture these past six weeks? How can a friend help you continue to memorize Scripture? How can you select other verses to memorize?**

Challenge students to continue to memorize at least one verse a week.

Step 2 Please Help Me! (20 min.)
Ask a volunteer to write this week's study topic on the last finger of the hand visual (Five Helps in Doing Bible Study). Say: **Since you had five different helps to study this week, let's look at each help as a review.** Divide students into five teams. (Remember that one or two students can be a team.) Assign each team one day from week 6. Tell teams to present their information from their assigned day by either: making up a skit, presenting a commercial or infomercial, making

up a game, designing a mobile or other structure, preparing a demonstration.

Allow time to work, then call for each team's information.

Step 3 Express Yourself (20 min.)
Without using their books, test students on their six weeks of learning. First, call on different students to name the items related to the five fingers of a hand. Next, ask students to identify the two rules to guide Bible study and the ten related guidelines. Ask other students to identify the three ways to do Bible study. Call on students to name the four areas of application. Finally, review the five helps in doing Bible study. (These are reviewed at the end of week 6, day 5.)

Point out the colored construction paper strips. Ask students to choose a color that expresses how they feel about this six-week study. Call on volunteers to share why they chose the colors they did.

Tell students to look at week 2, day 1. Direct them to the questions towards the end of that day ("Why do you want to study the Bible? Why do you want to understand what you study? How do you expect your life to be changed by what you read?") Call on volunteers to share their original answers to these questions. Ask: **How did those answers change during this six weeks of study? What did you expect to accomplish during this study? Did you accomplish what you wanted to? What one Bible study tool (commentary, concordance, etc.) has helped you the most? How? What one method (big picture, close-up, biographical, character trait, devotional, etc.) has most interested you? Why?**

Again, direct students to look at the colored construction paper strips and select a color that identifies a hope or a promise or a commitment that they have about future Bible study. Encourage volunteers to share their color selections and explain their choices.

Step 4 Ask, Seek, and Knock (5 min.)
Close the session by leading students to repeat this week's Scripture memory passage *(Matt. 7:7)*.

Pray a directed prayer (verbally guiding students through a time of prayer). As you pray, urge students to share their responses out loud. Say: **Jesus said that we could ask in His name and it would be so. Name someone or something that you are asking from God.** (Pause for students to respond, if they choose.) **SEEK: Seeking involves persistent asking. You may not get an instant answer, so you seek. What are you seeking? An understanding? A new emotion or attitude?** (Pause for students to respond, if they choose.) **KNOCK: Knocking implies persistent concern. You continue to pray for this situation or person until you get an answer from God. What keeps you totally committed in prayer?** (Pause for students to respond, if they choose.)
Amen.